REGULATIONS

AFFECTING INTERNATIONAL BANKING OPERATIONS OF BANK AND NON-BANKS

IN
BELGIUM-LUXEMBOURG
FRANCE
GERMANY
THE NETHERLANDS
SWEDEN
SWITZERLAND
THE UNITED KINGDOM

1981-1

ORGANISATION FOR ECONOMIC CO-OPERATION AND DEVELOPMENT

The Organisation for Economic Co-operation and Development (OECD) was set up under a Convention signed in Paris on 14th December 1960, which provides that the OECD shall promote policies designed:
- to achieve the highest sustainable economic growth and employment and a rising standard of living in Member countries, while maintaining financial stability, and thus to contribute to the development of the world economy;
- to contribute to sound economic expansion in Member as well as non-member countries in the process of economic development;
- to contribute to the expansion of world trade on a multilateral, non-discriminatory basis in accordance with international obligations.

The Members of OECD are Australia, Austria, Belgium, Canada, Denmark, Finland, France, the Federal Republic of Germany, Greece, Iceland, Ireland, Italy, Japan, Luxembourg, the Netherlands, New Zealand, Norway, Portugal, Spain, Sweden, Switzerland, Turkey, the United Kingdom and the United States.

Publié en français sous le titre:

RÉGLEMENTATIONS
TOUCHANT LES OPÉRATIONS BANCAIRES INTERNATIONALES

*
* *

FOREWORD

The papers in this volume have been prepared in close
co-operation between the OECD Secretariat and national experts, at
the request of the Committee on Financial Markets. Partly they are
an update of material that has appeared in an earlier volume with the
same title, published in 1978, to which papers on the regulatory
systems in some other countries have been added. Papers on regulations in some other OECD countries not included in the present
volume will be published separately at a later date.

The volume is published under the responsibility of the
Secretary-General and the views expressed therein are not necessarily
those of the Organisation for Economic Co-operation and Development
or its Member governments. The publication was authorised by the
OECD Council under the Organisation's Publication Programme for the
year 1980.

ALSO AVAILABLE

OECD FINANCIAL STATISTICS

This publication provides a unique collection of statistical and descriptive data on the international financial market and the national financial markets of 17 European countries, Australia, the United States, Canada and Japan.

The data are derived from more than 120 national and international sources in fourteen languages and are rendered as comparable as possible. Together with other data which have been specially compiled and are not published elsewhere, they are presented in tables which have been standardized as far as the individual features of the various financial markets permit at the present stage.

New formula as from October 1980:

Part 1. Financial Statistics Monthly

The most authoritative and the most up-to-date (2 weeks time-lag) data on the international and national financial markets:
— 350 interest rates;
— details on the Euro-bond and traditional foreign bond issues, on the medium- and long-term international bank loans and on the security issues on the domestic markets.

570 pages per year.

Part 2. Financial Accounts of OECD Countries

Flow-of-funds and balance-sheet accounts for 20 countries, detailed by sectors and by financial instruments. Integrated in an overall framework compatible with the concepts employed in the United Nations System of National Accounts.

Annual data published in 3 volumes as soon as available (940 pages per year).

Part 3. Non-financial Enterprises Financial Statement

Balance-sheets, statement of income and sources and uses of funds for a representative sample of companies in 12 countries.

Once a year (90 pages).

Methodological Supplement

Groups together the methodological notes of all the statistics reproduced in the Parts 1 to 3. These notes facilitate the interpretation of the statistics by describing their methods of calculation and the institutional context.

Once a year (200 pages).

Annual subscription to OECD Financial Statistics: F320, £35.40, US$80. Annual subscription to Financial Market Trends: F80, £8.90, US$20. Combined subscription to Financial Market Trends and to Financial Statistics Monthly: F220, £24.40, US$55.

CONTENTS

5

REGULATIONS AFFECTING INTERNATIONAL BANKING OPERATIONS[1] OF BANKS AND NON-BANKS IN SELECTED OECD COUNTRIES

General Introduction

The Committee on Financial Markets reviews regularly developments in the various segments of the international financial market and in the domestic capital markets of Member countries.

While primarily concerned with the market for long- and medium term securities, the Committee has also to take into account in its analyses the behaviour of money and credit markets, including the euro-currency and euro-credit markets, which have a strong impact on developments in international and domestic securities markets.

In order to assess the complex and fluid relationships between these various international and national markets, it is necessary to have a detailed knowledge of the regulatory frameworks applied by the main countries to international capital transactions through which their markets communicate with each other and with the euro-markets. In spite of the vast amount of literature published on the euro-markets and international banking operations generally, it appears that a comprehensive survey of such regulatory frameworks is not available.

The Committee therefore thought it useful to carry out such a survey and to make it available to the public. This is the main purpose of the present publication containing seven country notes - on Belgium/Luxembourg, France, Germany, the Netherlands, Sweden, Switzerland and the United Kingdom. The following plan is used in each of the country notes.

Section I contains a brief exposé of the main purposes of the regulatory system of the country concerned and a sub-section with selected data on related international banking operations.

Section II describes how the regulatory system affects various types of international short- and medium-term banking transactions, distinguishing between those carried out by banks (in foreign currencies and in domestic currency) and by non-banks to the extent that they operate with foreign banks or carry out transactions in foreign currencies also with domestic banks (see also Annex I).

---

[1] The term "banking operation" refers to capital transactions in which at least one contracting party is a bank; for more explanatory detail see Annex I.

Section III contains a synoptic tabulation of regulations applied, and instruments used, by the country, classified in matrix form by balance-sheet items, or by transactions, and according to six categories of regulations or instruments:

1) exchange control measures and similar devices;
2) minimum reserve requirements;
3) interest rate control;
4) prudential regulations;
5) tax regulations;
6) other regulations and intervention instruments.

Some of these regulations are not specifically aimed at influencing capital flows and are not flexibly modified for that purpose. Nevertheless, they may have an important bearing on shaping the country's position vis-à-vis euro-markets and foreign national markets. On the other hand, the notes do not discuss general policy instruments such as the domestic interest-rate or exchange-rate policy although they may have significant effects on capital flows.

Since the description of the regulatory framework is a main feature of the reports, the following explanations of the categories of regulations may be in order:

The first category (exchange controls) covers not only exchange controls in the legal sense of regulations laid down in an exchange control act or similar law but also other forms of administrative arrangement such as gentlement's agreements aimed at quantitative controls of capital movements.

The second category (minimum reserve requirements) refers to reserve ratio schemes applying to commercial banks which are operated in many countries in one form or another and also to similar ratio schemes which may be imposed on capital operations of the non-bank sector.

The third category (interest rate controls) includes any regulations or agreements applying to interest payments on financial instruments listed in the matrix, such as the imposition of ceilings on interest rates, the prohibition of interest payments or the imposition of penalty rates on certain financial assets. Interest-rate measures of a general nature, such as discount-rate changes, are not mentioned, however.

The fourth category (prudential regulations) cover measures specifically designed to improve the protection of depositors by limiting commercial banks' foreign-exchange risk exposure. Other prudential regulations, such as the imposition of certain balance-sheet ratios (deposit-to-capital ratio, long-term assets-to-capital

8

ratio, etc.) of a more general nature or limitations of the size of loans to individual borrowers, are not included, though in particular cases the observation of such regulations by individual banks may represent an obstacle to an intended expansion of euro-market business or other international banking operations.

In the fifth category (tax regulations) only taxes which directly affect interest payments on bank deposits or other bank liabilities, i.e. essentially withholding taxes, are noted. Other taxes, for example corporate taxes applying to commercial banks which may influence commercial banks' decisions concerning the choice of local euro-market centres in which they prefer to operate, are not considered.

All other regulations and administrative arrangements which cannot be classified under items I to V are included under item VI; for example, the use of special central bank swap facilities for influencing capital flows in one or another direction or quantitative limitations on domestic credit expansion which may also apply to euro-credits granted by banks to their resident clients. Excluded from the scope of the study are any requirements concerning the establishment of foreign-owned banks in Member countries. Such requirements may have a bearing on the development of local euro-market centres, despite the fact that the regulations examined in the ten countries are applied indiscriminately to both domestic and foreign-owned banks.

It should be noted that this classification of regulations by certain categories which may be somewhat arbitrary in some cases, follows essentially technical, and not necessarily legal, criteria. Thus, the material cannot be used for descriptions of, or for drawing conclusions on, the precise scope of particular laws in a given country (Foreign Exchange Act, Banking Act, etc.). The intention is rather to provide a guide which will facilitate the reader's understanding of the technical nature of Member countries' regulatory systems affecting international banking operations, notably euro-market operations of banks and non-banks in these countries and hence provide insight into the actual working of the euro-markets.

Section IV of each note expands the synoptic presentation of Section III by describing in some detail the regulations and instruments used by the country.

Section V contains a short list of references to the legal sources in which the regulations covered in the country notes are laid down.

Every effort has been made, with the help of the national authorities, to give a complete and accurate picture. Remaining errors and inaccuracies are the responsibility of the Secretariat.

The situation described is that existing towards the end of 1980 and the description will thus provide a bench-mark for a better understanding of future modifications. It is intended that revised versions of the country notes will be published from time to time.

The volume ends with two annexes containing notes on definitions, concepts and terminology used in the country reports (Annex I), and selected data on international banking showing in synoptic form the data material used for each country note (Annex II).

BELGIUM/LUXEMBOURG

I. INTRODUCTION

i) Main characteristics of the regulatory system

The main purpose of the regulations applicable to international banking transactions is to protect foreign exchange reserves against certain undesirable capital movements.

This was the specific purpose for which a two-tier foreign exchange market was set up in the Belgium-Luxembourg Economic Union: a controlled market reserved for current-account transactions and a free market for capital movements. The existence of a free market, in which the central bank does not intervene and where exchange rates may fluctuate without restriction, prevents capital movements from affecting foreign currency reserves.

Exchange controls, which are identical for both Belgium and Luxembourg, were devised so as to present no obstruction to current payments with foreign countries. Basically, the purpose of the controls is to channel payments into one or other of the markets according to the nature of the transactions involved.

During periods of strain on foreign exchange markets, however, some payments relating to external current transactions may be of a speculative kind, or at the very least, a form of risk covering; this is the case with "leads and lags", with changes in the spot positions of banks, and in Belgium or Luxembourg franc holdings on non-resident convertible franc accounts.

Concerning payments for imports and exports, the Belgium-Luxembourg Foreign Exchange Institute (Institut belgo-luxembourgeois du Change - I.B.L.C.) closely supervises the enforcement of its rules which stipulate that such payments must be made not more than three months before, or six months after, the date at which the goods go through customs.

The taking up by banks of uncovered foreign exchange positions in excess of their normal requirements for financing foreign trade has the disadvantage that it raises or lowers the external holdings of the National Bank of Belgium. Limits on the banks' positions are imposed by the I.B.L.C. to minimise this drawback.

Movements on non-resident convertible Belgian or Luxembourg franc holdings have to be free from restrictions, or else the convertibility of these holdings would be lost. This is why the authorities seek to influence such short-term international transfers and the adverse effects they have on foreign currency reserves. The authorities in Belgium use their credit policy for this purpose, while the Luxembourg authorities take such steps as are necessary in order not to hamper the Belgian measures.

Thus, the interest rates of the National Bank of Belgium are adjusted from time to time in order to maintain interest rates in general at a level which will limit the destabilizing effects of capital movements.

In October 1978 the Belgian monetary authorities used direct control of credit expansion in support of their foreign exchange policy. They realised that previous foreign exchange crises had been aggravated by short-term capital movements, especially in the form of commercial external claims created by enterprises in the course of foreign trade transactions, and they therefore laid down limits for the expansion of short-term credit to enterprises.

The same concern for safeguarding foreign reserves is seen in the requirement laid down in Belgium, in 1976 and in 1978, for financial intermediaries to maintain their holdings of government bills and securities at a certain level. This requirement was designed to support the official policy of liquidity restrictions and high interest rates which might otherwise have been made ineffective by the possibility for financial intermediaries of selling such bills and securities to offset the tightening of their liquidity.

Similar concerns prompted the Belgian and Luxembourg authorities to empower the I.B.L.C. in 1978 to restrict or forbid the remuneration of non-resident foreign currency holdings, to restrict foreign currency claims on non-residents and foreign currency liabilities to non-residents and to require intermediaries to deposit funds, to an amount equivalent to all or part of such claims or liabilities, in a blocked account.

On the other hand, both the surveillance of foreign exchange transaction of banks by the supervisory authorities (the Banking Commission in Belgium and the Commissariat for Banking Supervision in Luxembourg) and the tax provisions in Belgium relating to interest on foreign currency deposits of non-residents are for specific purposes altogether separate from the protection of foreign currency reserves.

ii)   Selected data on international banking operations

a) Belgium

If foreign liabilities in foreign currency are taken as the
criterion for ranking Euromarket centres, Belgium lies in fifth place
behind the United Kingdom, France, Luxembourg and the Netherlands
and ahead of Italy and Switzerland. In Belgium, at the end of 1979,
such liabilities amounted to $ 43.5 billion, equivalent to 6.5 per cent
of total liabilities of this kind of the twelve European countries
reporting to the Bank for International Settlements.

Transactions with non-residents, chiefly in foreign currency,
account for a substantial and increasing share in overall banking business. External assets at the end of 1979 accounted for 42.7 per cent
of the banks' consolidated balance sheet total - as against 32.1 per
cent at the end of 1970 - and external liabilities accounted for
49 per cent of the total, as against 37.5 per cent at the end of 1970.

Euromarket activity by Belgian banks basically consists of interbank transactions either amongst themselves or with banks in other
Euromarket centres.

At the end of 1979 foreign exchange assets of Belgian bankers
on the inter-bank market accounted for 70.7 per cent - as against
59.3 per cent at the end of 1970 - of their total claims in foreign
currency, while their foreign exchange liabilities on the inter-bank
market were equivalent to 87.5 per cent - as against 82.6 per cent at
the end of 1970 - of their total liabilities in foreign currency.

The role of the Belgian franc as a Euro-currency is almost neg-
ligible: aggregate net Belgian Franc external liabilities were equivalent to only about $ 3.3 billion (liabilities less assets at the end
of 1979).

b) Luxembourg

At the end of 1979, external foreign currency holdings by
Luxembourg banks came to 79.4 billion, of which 38.7 billion were with
non-banks, while foreign liabilities in foreign currency of these banks
amounted to 75.6 billion, of which 9.6 were to non-banks. Thus, amongst
the countries surveyed by the BIS, Luxembourg holds third place according to size on the Euromarket, with 12.4 per cent of assets and 11.4
per cent of liabilities, while on a net basis, excluding inter-bank
transactions, it even ranks second with 24.7 per cent of assets and
11 per cent of liabilities.

Transactions in foreign currency and with non-residents make up by far the largest proportion of transactions by Luxembourg banks. The proportion of foreign currency in the balance sheet aggregate for banks is in excess of 85 per cent, and where relations with non-banks are concerned more than 90 per cent of assets and more than 70 per cent of liabilities are external.

Euro-currency market activities by Luxembourg banks show a strong geographical bias towards OECD countries, as well as the characteristic strength of the DM amongst the currencies employed, ranking it equal with the dollar which in other Euromarket centres is much more preponderant over other currencies. Similarly, the presence of Luxembourg institutions on the Eurobond market is quite sizeable.

II. ANALYSIS OF REGULATIONS BY MAIN TYPES OF CAPITAL MOVEMENTS

(situation at the end of 1980)

i)   Commercial banks' foreign currency operations

a) External foreign currency borrowing for re-lending abroad

- Exchange control

There are no restrictions on this type of transaction, provided foreign currency amounts borrowed are recorded by the banks amongst their "free" holdings.

- Exchange control, interest rate restrictions and minimum reserve requirements

Nevertheless, the Law of 20th December 1974 and implementing order of 18th July 1978 in Belgium, and likewise the Law of 31st March 1978 and implementing regulation of 13th April, 1978 in Luxembourg enable the authorities to influence the trend in such banking transactions. The Belgium-Luxembourg Exchange Institute (I.B.L.C.) may if the need arises impose regulations directed at banks and traders regularly carrying on business with abroad, and designed to:

. limit or prohibit the renumeration of non-residents foreign currency holdings;

. limit foreign currency claims on non-residents and foreign currency liabilities to non-residents;

. make it compulsory for funds of an amount equivalent to all or part of the aforementioned claims and liabilities to be deposited in a blocked account.

To date the I.B.L.C. has not made any use of its powers under these regulations.

14

Tax regulations

Tax at twenty per cent (the "précompte mobilier" or withholding tax) is deducted at source on interest income credited, paid or received in Belgium. However, the withholding tax does not apply, in particular, to income from credits and loans paid by banks established in Belgium to banks established abroad, nor to income from credits and loans for which no bearer securities are issued and which is paid or credited by banks established in Belgium to non-resident savers, provided such savers have not used their investment capital for business purposes in Belgium.

b) Capital inflows via inward switching

- Exchange control

Banks may freely convert foreign currency holdings into francs. Transactions of this kind may be carried out with or without forward cover.

However, foreign currency positions of banks in the controlled market are subject to the I.B.L.C. instructions of 18th June, 1976:

- . As a rule, banks may not take up an overall long or short position (spot and forward taken together) in foreign currencies on the controlled market. Banks are allowed some leeway in order to unwind on a day-to-day basis the transactions they have in hand.

- . As a rule, no single bank may have a spot long or short position in foreign currency on the controlled market in excess of 20 million Belgian francs. Higher individual ceilings have been set for the major banks, to take account of the overall volume of their operations. In addition, in order not to disturb the normal course of operations, the I.B.L.C. allows the set limit to be temporarily exceeded by not more than ten per cent.

c) Capital inflows via the use of foreign-currency funds raised abroad for granting foreign-currency loans to resident non-banks

- Exchange control

Banks may freely grant foreign-currency loans to resident non-banks. No restrictions apply where the proceeds of such loans are used to finance expenditure in the B.L.E.U. or to finance external transactions to be settled on the free market. In the latter case banks are merely required to record such transactions with their "free" holdings. On the other hand, where the loans are used to finance external transactions for which settlement is to be made on the controlled market, banks

15

must record such transactions on their "controlled market" position, and the foreign currency lent must be used immediately by the borrower to cover an authorised transaction.

- Tax regulations

Tax at 20 per cent ("précompte mobilier") is deducted at source on income from securities paid, credited or received in Belgium. However, the withholding tax does not apply, in particular, to income from credits and loans paid by banks established in Belgium to banks established abroad, nor to income from credits and loans for which bearer securities are not issued and which is paid or credited by banks established in Belgium to non-resident savers, provided such savers have not used their investment capital for business purposes in Belgium.

d) Capital outflows via outward switching

- Exchange control

Banks may freely convert their franc holding into foreign currency on the free market, with or without forward cover.

Where holdings in francs are converted into a foreign currency on the controlled market, the I.B.L.C. instructions of 18th June 1976 apply: see Section (b) above.

- Exchange control and minimum reserve requirements

The law of 20th September, 1974 and implementing order of 18th July 1978, for Belgium, and the law of 31st March 1978 and implementing regulation of 13th April 1978 in Luxembourg should allow some measure of control over such transactions, by:

. restricting foreign currency bank claims on non-residents;

. requiring banks to deposit funds to an amount equivalent to all or part of such claims in a blocked account.

e) Capital outflows via financing external foreign currency assets with foreign currency deposits from resident non-banks

- Exchange control

Resident non-banks are free to deposit foreign currency with banks in the B.L.E.U., provided the amounts deposited were purchased on the free market

Resident non-banks may however keep with a bank and in foreign currency the proceeds of their exports of goods and services, on special "controlled" accounts which may subsequently be used only for current external payments. Balances on such accounts may earn interest.

From this it follows that residents may only constitute reserves to cover subsequent payments for imports of goods and services in foreign currency by using their receipts from exports.

In these circumstances, there is little incentive for resident non-banks to deposit holdings in foreign currency in "controlled" accounts with B.L.E.U. banks.

- Tax regulations

Interest on resident non-bank deposits in foreign currency with banks in Belgium is taxable at source at 20 per cent ("précompte mobilier"), except where the depositors are parastatal social security institutions or institutions of similar status.

ii)   Commercial banks' domestic-currency operations with non-residents

f) Domestic currency liabilities to non-residents

- Exchange control

The consequence of the two-tier foreign exchange market in the B.L.E.U. is that non-resident domestic currency accounts with banks in the Economic Union are divided into two types.

a) Convertible accounts are intended to record payments in francs relating to transactions on the controlled market. They may be credited with the proceeds of sale of foreign currency on the controlled market and are convertible into foreign currency on that market.

b) Financial accounts are intended to record payment in francs for transactions on the free market. They may be credited with the proceeds of sale of foreign currency on the free market, or with bank-notes, and are convertible into foreign currency on the free market and can be used for cash withdrawals.

Transfers between these two types of account are forbidden.

- Tax regulations

a) Tax at 20 per cent ("précompte mobilier") is deducted at source on income from securities paid, credited or received in Belgium. However, the withholding tax does not apply, in particular, to income from credits and loans paid by banks established in Belgium to banks established abroad, nor to income from credits and loans for which bearer securities are not issued and which is paid or credited by banks established in Belgium to non-resident savers, provided such savers have not used their investment capital for business purposes in Belgium.

b) In exceptional circumstances, tax may be charged on non-resident Belgian franc and foreign currency deposits with B.L.E.U. banks.

- Exchange control, minimum reserve requirements and interest rate controls

The law of 20th December 1974 and implementing order of 18th July 1978 in Belgium, the law of 31st March 1978 and implementing regulation of 13th April 1978 in Luxembourg, give the I.B.L.C. powers (which have not yet been invoked):

. to restrict or prohibit remuneration of non-residents franc or foreign currency holdings;

. to impose a ceiling on such holdings;

. to require funds, to an amount equivalent to all or part of the bank's franc and foreign currency liabilities to non-residents, to be deposited in a blocked account.

Before these powers were conferred under the foregoing statutes, the Belgian authorities:

. prohibited remuneration of non-resident convertible accounts between 11th May 1971 and 28th January 1974, under the general exchange control regulations;

. under an agreement with the banks, caused a special commission to be charged on increases in holdings on non-resident accounts, between 26th March and 31st July 1973 and between 1st October and 31st December 1973

. required a monetary reserve to be constituted with the National Bank of Belgium, between 26th July 1972 and 19th May 1975, with reserve ratios applying to both the amount of and increases in liabilities of banks to non-resident convertible account-holders, varying according to economic conditions;

. made an agreement with the banks in October 1976 under which, in an economic crisis, a special rate of interest is chargeable on non-resident convertible-account advances to the banks' correspondent bankers.

- The Luxembourg authorities brought in similar measures between those same dates.

g) Placing of domestic-currency funds with foreign banks

- Exchange control

Banks are free to place funds in this way and hence to feed francs into the Euromarket.

h) Domestic-currency credits and loans to non-residents
   non-banks

- Exchange control

Banks are free to grant such credits and loans on financial accounts with the reservation that the proceeds cannot be used to effect settlements through the controlled foreign exchange market.

Credits on convertible accounts may take the form of overdrafts for a period not exceeding a reasonable period of delay in mailing.

In 1978, the Belgian National Bank curbed expansion in outstanding bank credit by setting limits to the growth of such lending by Belgian financial intermediaries in order to prevent the rapid accumulation of short-term external assets in the course of foreign trade operations.

It was for the same purpose that in 1976 and 1978 the National Bank of Belgium laid down the requirement for Belgian financial intermediaries to maintain their holdings of government bills and securities at a certain level.

An agreement has been in existence since October 1976 between the National Bank of Belgium and the banks under which, during periods of economic crisis, a special rate of interest is chargeable on convertible account advances to the banks' non-resident correspondent bankers. This rate is based on the real cost of the convertible Belgian franc as derived from the forward exchange rate for the convertible Belgian franc, on a daily basis. In such circumstances the same rate is chargeable by the Luxembourg banks.

iii)   Non-bank borrowing and lending operations with non-resident banks

   j) Capital inflows via borrowing from non-resident banks

   - Exchange Control

There is no restriction in external borrowing in foreign currency by non-bank residents. However, they may only convert such funds into francs on the free market.

External borrowing in francs is likewise unrestricted provided that it is by debit of financial accounts.

- Tax regulations

Tax at 20 per cent ("précompte mobilier") is deducted at source on income paid or credited in Belgium.

k) Capital outflows via placing of liquid assets with non-resident banks

- Exchange control

Resident non-banks are free to place foreign currency liquid assets which they have acquired on the free foreign exchange market with non-resident banks.

The placing of assets in francs, through "financial" accounts, is likewise unrestricted.

- Tax regulations

Tax at 20 per cent ("précompte mobilier") is deducted at source on income received through a Belgian intermediary, except where the beneficiary is a parastatal social security or similar institution (in the case of borrowing, claims, loans and deposits) or an individual or legal entity using his/its investment capital for business purposes (in the case of debts and loans only).

III. SUMMARY VIEW OF REGULATIONS AND INSTRUMENTS AFFECTING INTERNATIONAL BANKING OPERATIONS OF BANKS AND NON-BANKS IN

BELGIUM/LUXEMBOURG

(situation at the end of 1980)

Type of Operation or Balance Sheet Position / Type of Regulation or Instrument	Code	I. Exchange Control (1)	II. Minimum Reserve Requirements	III. Interest Rate Control	IV. Prudential Regulations	V. Tax Regulations	VI. Other Regulations or instruments
COMMERCIAL BANKS	1.						
Liability Operations/Positions	11.					x	
in foreign currencies	11.1				x		
with non-residents	11.11	x	x	x		x	
deposits from	11.111						
banks	11.111.1					x	
non-banks	11.111.2					x	
credits and loans from	11.112						
banks	11.112.1					x	
non-banks	11.112.2					x	
fixed-interest	11.113					x	
securities							
money market paper	11.113.1						
bonds	11.113.2						
with residents	11.12	x	x	x			
deposits from	11.121						
banks	11.121.1						
non-banks	11.121.2						
Central Bank or Government	11.121.3					x	
in domestic currency	11.2						
with non-residents	11.21	x	x	x		x	
current accounts of	11.211						
banks	11.211.1					x	
non-banks	11.211.2					x	
time deposits from	11.212						
banks	11.212.1					x	
non-banks	11.212.2					x	
credits and loans from	11.213						
banks	11.213.1					x	
non-banks	11.213.2					x	
fixed-interest securities	11.214					x	
money market paper	11.214.1						
bonds	11.214.2						
Asset Operations/Positions	12.						
in foreign currencies	12.1				x		
with non-residents	12.11	x	x				
banks	12.111						
current accounts	12.111.1						
time deposits	12.111.2						
credits and loans	12.111.3						
non-banks	12.112						
credits and loans	12.112.1						
securities	12.113						
with residents	12.12	x	x				
deposits with banks	12.121						
credits and loans to non-banks	12.122						
securities	12.123						
deposits with Central bank	12.124						

(1) And similar regulations imposing quantitative controls on capital transactions with non-residents.

III. SUMMARY VIEW OF REGULATIONS AND INSTRUMENTS AFFECTING INTERNATIONAL BANKING OPERATIONS OF BANKS AND NON-BANKS IN

(Continued)

BELGIUM/LUXEMBOURG

(situation at the end of 1980)

Type of Operation or Balance Sheet Position / Type of Regulation or Instrument	Code	I. Exchange Control (1)	II. Minimum Reserve Requirements	III. Interest Rate Control	IV. Prudential Regulations	V. Tax Regulations	VI. Other Regulations or instruments
in domestic currency	12.2						
with non-residents	12.21	x	x				
deposits with banks	12.211						
credits and loans to	12.212			x			
banks	12.212.1						
non-banks	12.212.2						
securities	12.213						
Net Positions	13.	x					
in foreign currencies	13.1						
vis-à-vis non-residents	13.2						
NON-BANKS	2.						
Liability Operations/ Positions	21.						
credits and loans from	21.1						
non-resident banks	21.11						
in foreign currencies	21.111	x					
in domestic currency	21.112	x					
resident banks	21.12						
in foreign currencies	21.121	x					
Asset Operations/Positions	22.						
with non-resident banks	22.1						
in foreign currencies	22.11	x					
current accounts	22.111						
time deposits	22.112						
in domestic currency	22.12	x					
deposits	22.121						
with resident banks	22.2						
in foreign currencies	22.21	x					
current accounts	22.211						
time deposits	22.212						
FOREIGN EXCHANGE OPERATIONS/ POSITIONS	3.						
Commercial Banks	31.						
spot foreign exchange dealings	31.1	x					
forward foreign exchange dealings	31.2	x					
swap transactions	31.3	x					
net foreign exchange positions	31.4	x					
Non-Banks	32.						
spot foreign exchange dealings	32.1	x					
forward foreign exchange dealings	32.2	x					
swap transactions	32.3	x					

(1) And similar regulations imposing quantitative controls on capital transactions with non-residents.

22

IV. LISTING OF REGULATIONS BY CATEGORIES AND BY OPERATIONS
ON BALANCE SHEET POSITIONS

(situation at the end of March 1980)

CODE NO. OF CLASSIFICATION SCHEMA	OPERATION/POSITION	REGULATION
	I. EXCHANGE CONTROL <u>Commercial banks</u>	
11.	<u>Liabilities</u>	
11.11	Commercial banks' foreign currency liabilities to non-residents	Banks may take in all foreign-currency deposits from external depositors and may borrow foreign currency abroad. The I.B.L.C. may, if the need arises, impose regulations on the banks limiting the amount of their foreign currency liabilities to non-residents.
11.12	Commercial banks' foreign currency liabilities to residents	Such liabilities may be entered into without restriction provided the foreign currency has been purchased on the free market. On the controlled market, banks may only commit themselves to the extent provided under exchange control regulations, i.e. "controlled" foreign currency accounts for residents who have received such currency in payment for the export of goods and services.
11.21	Commercial banks' franc liabilities to non-residents	Such liabilities may be entered into with without restriction so long as the francs are paid into a convertible or financial account in accordance with the general exchange control rules. The I.B.L.C. I.B.L.C. may, if the need arises, impose regulations on the banks limiting the amount of their Belgian franc liabilities to non-residents.

23

CODE No. OF CLASSIFICATION SCHEMA	OPERATION/POSITION	REGULATION
	Claims	
12.11	Commercial banks' foreign currency claims on non-residents	Such claims may be freely constituted provided the relevant operations take place on the free market. Where they take place on the controlled market, only short-term placings are allowed. The I.B.L.C. may, if the need arises, impose regulations on the banks limiting the amount of their foreign currency claims on non-residents.
12.12	Commercial banks' foreign currency claims on residents	There are no restrictions governing the constitution of such claims where bank loans are used to finance expenditure in the B.L.E.U. or to finance external transactions to be settled on the free market. Such claims must be recorded by the banks among their "free" assets.
		Where bank loans are intended to finance external transactions to be settled on the controlled market, the banks must record the corresponding claims among their "controlled" assets, and the borrower must use the foreign currency immediately for payment.
		The I.B.L.C. may, if the need arises, impose regulations on the banks limiting the amount of their foreign currency claims on residents.
12.21	Commercial banks' domestic currency claims on non-residents	The banks are free to make any type of advance on "financial" accounts without requiring authorisation. They may do so on convertible accounts only where the claims arise from overdrafts not exceeding a reasonable period of delays in mailing.
		The I.B.L.C. may, if the need arises, impose regulations on the banks limiting the amount of their Belgian franc claims on non-residents.
13.	Commercial banks' net foreign currency positions vis-à-vis non-residents	See item 31.4.
2.	Non-banks	
21.	Liabilities	
21.11	Non-banks' liabilities to non-resident banks	

CODE No. OF CLASSIFICATION SCHEMA	OPERATION/POSITION	REGULATION
21.111	In foreign currency	Such liabilities may be entered into where the credits and loans received are used to finance expenditure in the B.L.E.U. or to finance external transactions to be settled on the free market.
21.112	In francs	Such liabilities may be freely entered into provided that the amounts borrowed are transferred by debit of a "financial" account in the name of the foreign creditor.
21.121	Non-banks' foreign currency liabilities to resident banks	Such liabilities may be freely entered into, provided that the banks record any foreign currency so acquired among their "free" assets. However, resident non-banks may borrow foreign currency to make current-account payments within the controlled market, provided that the proceeds of such borrowing are used immediately.
22.	Claims	
22.1	Non-banks' claims on non-resident banks	
22.11	In foreign currency	Such claims may be freely constituted provided that the foreign currency is purchased on the free market.
22.12	In domestic currency	Such claims may be freely constituted provided that any settlement in connection with them is made through a "financial" account.
22.21	Non-banks' foreign currency claims on resident banks	Such claims may be freely constituted provided that the foreign currency acquired in connection with such claims and placed with resident banks is recorded by them among their "free" assets. However, resident bon-banks may deposit foreign currency received in payment for current operations(on the controlled market) in the resident banks' special "controlled" accounts, which can be debited only for settlement of current transactions.
3.	Foreign exchange	
31.	Commercial banks	

CODE No. OF CLASSIFICATION SCHEMA	OPERATION/POSITION	REGULATION
31.1	Spot foreign exchange operations	Banks may carry out any operation on the free market. On the controlled market, they may carry out only those operations expressly provided for in the foreign exchange regulations.
31.2	Forward foreign exchange operations	Banks may carry out any operation on the free market. On the controlled market, they may carry out only those operations expressly provided for in the foreign exchange regulations.
31.3	Swap operations	There is no restriction on these operations, provided they are carried out on the free foreign exchange market. However, banks may conduct such transactions on the controlled market to meet their operating needs and their and their customers' requirements.
31.4	Commercial banks' net foreign currency position	Banks may not take up an overall "long" or "short" foreign currency position (spot and forward taken together) on the controlled market. However, the banks are allowed some latitude in order to unwind on a day-to-day basis the transactions they have in mind. As a rule, no single bank may take up a spot "long" or "short" foreign currency position on the controlled market in excess of 20 million Belgian francs. However, higher individual ceilings have been set for the major banks, to take account of the overall volume of their operations. In addition, in order not to disrupt the usual course of business, the I.B.L.C. allows the set limit to be temporarily exceeded by not more than 10 per cent.

In any case, from the exchange control point of view, there are no regulations governing the positions of banks on the free market. |
| 32. | Non-banks | |
| 32.1 | Spot foreign exchange operations | These operations may be carried out on the free market without restriction. |

CODE No. OF CLASSIFICATION SCHEMA	OPERATION/POSITION	REGULATION
32.2	Resident non-banks forward foreign exchange operations	Forward cover for financial operations must be effected on the free market.
		Forward cover for current operations is subject to certain requirements:
		- cover must be effected through an authorised bank;
		- external payments must be made within 15 working days from delivery, failing which the authorised bank must automatically repurchase unutilised foreign currency on the controlled market;
		- any profit on foreign exchange greater than Frs. 1,000 arising from non-fulfilment of the forward exchange contract and from the bank automatically re-purchasing unutilised foreign currency or from delivery to the bank of foreign currency purchased on the controlled market is automatically forfeited.
32.3	Swap operations	These transactions may be conducted without restriction on the free market.

II. Minimum reserve requirement

11.11 11.21	Commercial banks' foreign and domestic currency liabilities to non-residents	Where the circumstances require, the I.B.L.C. may lay down regulations for banks requiring them to deposit funds in a blocked account to an amount equivalent to all or part of:
		a) their foreign and domestic currency liabilities to non-residents
11.12	Commercial banks' foreign-currency liabilities to residents	b) their foreign-currency liabilities to residents
12.11 12.21	Commercial banks' foreign and domestic currency and claims on non-residents	c) their foreign and domestic currency claims on non-residents
12.12	Commercial banks' foreign-currency claims on residents	d) their foreign currency claims on residents

CODE No. OF CLASSIFI-CATION SCHEMA	OPERATION/POSITION	REGULATION
	III. Interest rate controls	
11.11 11.21	Commercial banks' foreign and domestic currency liabilities to non-residents	The I.B.L.C. may, if the need arises, lay down regulations for banks restricting or prohibiting the remuneration:- a) of non-residents' foreign and domestic currency balances;
11.12	Commercial banks' foreign currency liabilities to residents	b) of residents' foreign currency balances on "free" accounts Residents' foreign currency balances on "controlled accounts are already covered by the regulatory system. Such accounts may currently be remunerated. They must be kept as sight deposits, but this restriction will shortly be lifted.
12.212	Commercial banks' domestic currency claims on non residents	Since October 1976, under a gentlemen's agreement between the Belgian com-mercial banks and the National Bank of Belgium, the latter may require the banks to charge a special rate of interest on advances on external convertible accounts in the the event of tension on foreign exchange markets. In these circumstances the same rate is charged by the Luxembourg banks.
	IV. Prudential regulations for the protection of depositors	
11.1	Banks' foreign currency assets and liabilities	In Belgium, Royal Decree No. 185 of 9th July,1935 (last amended by the Law of 30th June 1975) empowers the Banking Commission to lay down for all banks, or by type of bank, the ratios to be observed between spot and forward foreign currency assets on the one hand and spot and forward foreign currency liabilities on the other and may do so where necessary, according to currency and maturity, or between some of those assets and liabilities (Article 11, d). The

CODE No. OF CLASSIFICATION SCHEMA	OPERATION/POSITION	REGULATION
		Commission may also set quantitative limits for some of these items. As regards ratios or quantitative limits, it may be the total of book items which may be subject to control, or changes in those items over a reference period, or both. Ratios and quantitative limits may be set on the basis of the consolidated position for a bank and its subsidiaries.
		On 13th June, 1972 under Article 11 of Royal Decree No. 185 of 1935, the Banking Commission issued regulations which, among other matters, treat a bank's "contingency reserves" as ""equity capital". Included in these reserves are 0.2 per cent of total receivables in Belgian francs and foreign currency on forward exchange transactions.
		In Luxembourg the Commissariat for Banking Supervision lays down no ratios for foreign currency assets and liabilities of banks. However, periodical reports are relied on to monitor changes in the foreign exchange position on the free market and the maturity structure of claims and liabilities.

V. Tax regulations

11.	Commercial banks' liabilities	Tax at 20 per cent deducted at source (the "précompte mobilier") is levied on income from debts and loans paid, credited, or received in Belgium.
11.111.1 11.112.1 11.113 11.211.1 11.212.1 11.213.1 11.214	Commercial banks' liabilities to non-resident banks	The 20 per cent tax deducted at source is not due a) on income from credits and loans paid by banks established in Belgium to banks established abroad;

CODE No. OF CLASSIFICATION SCHEMA	OPERATION/POSITION	REGULATION
11.111.2 11.112.2 11.211.2 11.212.2 11.213.2	Commercial banks' liabilities to non-resident non-banks	b) on income from credits and loans for which no bearer securities are issued paid by banks established in Belgium to non-resident savers, provided such savers have not used their investment capital for business purposes in Belgium;
11.121.3	Commercial banks' foreign currency liabilities to Belgian parastate institutions	c) on interest accruing to foreign currency deposits of parastatal social security or similar institutions
11.11 11.21	Banks' liabilities to non-residents	Tax may be levied on non-resident foreign currency and Belgian franc balances with banks in the B.L.E.U.

FRANCE

I. INTRODUCTION

i) Main features of the regulatory system

Over the last decade or so, the external payments situation of France and its exchange rate have repeatedly been subject to pressures resulting from current account deficits, which were particularly large between 1974 and 1977, and also at times from outflows of private capital. The only disruption France has experienced from inflows of capital was during brief spells in the early 1970s, when the dollar was under attack on foreign exchange markets and the French franc was maintaining a relatively strong position.

The basic aim of the authorities is, therefore, to maintain close control over outward movements of capital by residents and to restrict the scope for speculation against the French franc by both residents and non-residents. A distinctly more liberal attitude is taken towards capital inflows, although these could come under stricter control if this were considered necessary in furtherance of internal monetary policies. In order to influence the overall capital account of the balance-of-payments in the desired direction, the authorities make extensive use of exchange-control techniques.

With the conspicuous exception of resident purchases of securities abroad, practically all the channels for outward movement of capital(1) are either closed or strictly controlled. Issues of foreign securities on the domestic capital market are subject to controls and the issue of bonds is practically prohibited. Banks may have net asset positions in foreign currencies only to the extent that they have been authorised to purchase currency to increase their own holdings. Banks are not permitted to grant French franc loans abroad except for the financing of French exports of goods and services. Residents are not as a rule permitted to hold liquid assets with banks abroad, including holdings in Euro-francs.

_____

(1) Except direct investment.

A whole set of regulations is aimed at restricting resident and non-resident speculation against the franc. The prohibition of liquid external foreign-currency holdings by residents has already been mentioned, as has the control on banks' net foreign currency positions. Residents are required to repatriate and dispose of their foreign currency receipts within a very short period of time (currently 8 days). Advance payment for imports and forward foreign exchange cover are also subject to restrictions. To limit non-resident sales of French francs in exchange for foreign currencies, bank and non-bank French franc loans abroad other than in connection with export financing are forbidden. The Euro-franc market is cut off from all domestic supplies of funds.

Where capital imports are concerned, non-resident purchases of French securities, swap operations in which French banks lend in foreign currencies against francs (inward switching) and the contracting of trade loans abroad in foreign currency are not subject to any restrictions. However, all other kinds of borrowing, and external issues of bonds, are subject to control and are permitted only as balance-of-payments financing needs and the exigencies of domestic credit control allow.

Notwithstanding the tight control over the channels linking the domestic financial market with those abroad, French banks do play an important part as intermediaries on the Euro-market. They are permitted to borrow foreign currency abroad for onlending to non-residents (banks or enterprises). Transactions of this kind are not subject to reserve requirements, nor are they covered by any specific regulations regarding interest rates or taxation. Indeed, interest paid on non-resident foreign currency deposits is specifically exempted from French taxation at source.

ii)   Selected data on international banking operations

France is the second largest international financial centre in Europe after London, chiefly because of its banking system's activity on the Euro-markets, also in second place following the London market, whilst its international banking business in domestic currency remains very much less important on account of exchange controls and in line with government policy intentions.

External liabilities of French banks rose from 31.9 billion dollars at the end of 1973 to 106.2 billion dollars at the end of 1979, while France's share in the total external liabilities of banks in the European countries reporting to the Bank for International

Settlements amounted to 13.7 per cent at the end of 1979, as against 14.3 per cent at the end of 1973. On the other hand, France's position in terms of its Euro-market business has strengthened in the last few years, with its market share of total banking business on those markets increasing from 14.1 per cent to 15.0 per cent over the same period(1).

France has not made much use of its own banking system on the Euro-markets to raise capital abroad despite its heavy external financing needs in recent years. At the end of 1979, the banks reported a very small credit position ($ 0.84 billion) as against minor debt positions in 1973 ($ -0.27 billion) and 1976 ($ -0.67 billion).

In domestic currency, however, a sizeable credit position is observed ($ +16.6 billion in 1979) arising from the financing of French exports in francs. If however this item is excluded, the external French franc position of French banks usually shows a significant debit balance in line with the very stringent control over French franc loans to non-residents by French banks. Non-residents' French franc deposits with French banks at the end of 1979 amounted to the relatively low figure of $ 6.61 billion, presumably representing cash balances for making international settlements in French francs.

The importance of France's role as an international financial centre is also reflected in the banks' balance sheets, where foreign business accounted for 28.3 per cent and 24.0 per cent of assets and liabilities respectively at the end of 1979(2).

The French franc plays only a secondary role as a Euro-currency, in keeping with official policy aims. Euro-French franc deposits at the end of 1979 amounted only to the quivalent of $ 11.4 billion, or approximately 1.7 per cent of total Euro-currency liabilities, ranking it roughly equal with Euro-sterling or the Euro-guilder. Euro-franc holdings are chiefly maintained in Brussels and London

---

(1) Market share is reckoned as a percentage of the total foreign currency external liabilities of banks in the European countries (Belgium and Luxembourg being taken separately) reporting to the Bank for International Settlements.

(2) These percentages are derived from data published in the IMF International Financial Statistics on Deposit Money Banks which exclude domestic inter-bank deposits.

II. ANALYSIS OF REGULATIONS BY MAIN TYPES
OF CAPITAL MOVEMENTS

(situation at the end of 1980)

i) Commercial banks' foreign currency operations

a) External foreign currency borrowing for relending abroad

Commercial banks are free to accept foreign currency deposits,
or to borrow in foreign currency, from non-resident banks or non-
banks, and to deploy such funds abroad in the form of foreign currency
deposits with foreign banks, money market instruments or portfolio
investments, or loans to non-residents, including participation in
Euro-loan syndicates. There are no indirect restrictions on these
transactions, in the form of minimum reserve requirements on external
foreign currency deposits(1) interest-rate restrictions, or withholding
taxes(2), and there is no maturity constraints on external foreign
currency claims or liabilities. The only type of foreign currency
liability operation which is subject to prior authorisation by the
authorities is the issue of notes (including certificates of deposit)
and bonds abroad; and authorisation for such issues is, moreover, not
usually given.

b) Capital inflows via inward switching

Commercial banks are permitted to sell foreign currency in
exchange for francs, especially for the financing of French franc
credit facilities to residents. Banks are also authorised to purchase
foreign currency forward to cover the exchange risk arising from such
operations. However the scope for these capital movements is limited
by the fact that French franc credits granted under such conditions
come within the scope of internal monetary policy measures (credit
ceilings).

Commercial banks are allowed to sell foreign currency forward
in exchange for French francs. The Bank of France does not intervene
on the forward French franc market.

---

(1) Resident foreign currency deposits were temporarily subject to
    minimum reserve requirements from July to September 1968 at a
    ratio of 10 per cent; since then all foreign currency liabilities
    are excluded from minimum reserve.
(2) Interest payments on non-resident foreign currency deposits are
    specifically exempted from French withholding tax provisions.

Notwithstanding the regulatory controls over banks' foreign exchange positions, they can reduce their foreign currency credit balances or where the circumstances arise take a debit position.

c) Capital inflows via the use of foreign-currency funds raised abroad for granting foreign-currency loans to resident non-banks

Control by the authorities over this type of capital inflow is directed at foreign currency loans by banks to residents, which are subject to exchange control regulations. Three main types of advances or loans are distinguishable:

1. Foreign currency loans for the financing of imports and exports of goods and services (the execution of major works contracts abroad, engineering services etc.) and international trading in raw materials are permitted without limit and under general authorisation.

2. Also permitted under general authorisation are foreign-currency loans for domestic use under the following conditions:

   - the rate of interest must be the normal market rate;

   - the maturity must be not less than one year;

   - borrowing proceeds must be immediately transferred and sold on the foreign exchange market;

   - the amount of debt outstanding per borrower under this heading must not exceed the equivalent of Frs. 10 million

3. All other loans require special authorisation by the Ministry of the Economy (Direction du Trésor), including Euro-loans to French residents syndicated by international consortia in which French banks participate.

d) Capital outflows via outward switching

Capital outflows via purchases by banks of foreign currency in exchange for francs can only be of limited extent since, first, banks may only purchase currencies in exchange for francs if the transaction does not result in an increase in their foreign exchange position (or net position in foreign currency), and secondly, they may not enter into forward foreign exchange contracts with their foreign correspondents where the latter would be selling francs forward, and banks may enter into such forward contracts with their resident customers only on certain conditions. In practice only French importers are permitted to purchase foreign currencies forward, to pay for their

imports, and then only for a period restricted as a rule to two
months. This restriction is not applied in those cases where forward
cover is required for payment of imports of a specified list of goods.
The Bank of France does not intervene on the forward foreign exchange
market. Lastly, French banks are not permitted to purchase foreign
currency for lending either to residents or to non-residents.

e) Capital outflows via financing external foreign-currency
   assets with foreign-currency deposits from resident non-
   banks

There is limited scope for extending this type of capital
outflows since the regulatory system restricts holdings of foreign
currency deposits by residents. Importers purchasing foreign currency
to make payments abroad may not hold such foreign currency on deposit
with French banks for more than eight days. Similarly, residents
receiving payment in foreign currency from abroad may not keep such
foreign currency on deposit for more than eight days. Beyond that
period, unused foreign currency must be disposed of on the foreign
exchange market. Moreover, interest paid on such deposits is subject
to the normal tax regulations, i.e. profits tax or personal income tax,
though in the latter case the individual concerned may opt to be
taxed at a flat rate of 40 per cent(1). On the other hand, as regards
interest rates, the banks are free to offer Euro-market rates.

ii) Commercial banks' domestic currency operations with non-
    residents

f) Domestic-currency liabilities to non-residents

There are no restrictions, direct or indirect, on deposits in
French francs by non-residents with French banks(2)

_____

(1) Since 1980 this rate has been reduced to 38 per cent where deposits
    are held in the depositor's name and increased to 42 per cent
    where they are not.
(2) French banks do not borrow abroad in domestic currency (Euro-
    francs), because of adverse interest rate differentials.

Unlike resident accounts, all classes of non-resident French franc accounts may be remunerated at rates freely determined by the banks(1). Between 1974 and 1980, these accounts have been excluded; since 21st November, 1980, they are subject to a reserve requirement of 5 per cent. The only rule which can dissuade non-residents from building up French franc deposits with French banks (as opposed to Euro-French franc deposits with banks abroad is a tax regulation requiring a non-resident depositor to be charged withholding tax at the rate of 38 per cent or 42 per cent. However, the scope of this provision is moderated by virtue of the international double-taxation agreements France has entered into, whereby the rate is generally speaking reduced to 10 or 15 per cent. Moreover, this regulation does not apply to French franc holdings of foreign correspondent banks with French banks.

g) Placing domestic currency funds with foreign banks

The banks are not permitted to keep sight deposits or other claims in French francs with foreign banks, except for overdrafts on non-resident French franc accounts which may occur as a result of delays in mailing and must not exceed ten days ("mail credits").

h) Domestic currency credits and loans to non-resident non-banks

Banks may only grant to non-resident non-banks certain export credits or other special export-related credits, and mortgage loans or other credits to finance purchases by non-residents of dwellings or real estate for their personal use in France up to 50 per cent of the purchase price.

iii) Non-bank borrowing and lending operations with non-resident banks

j) Capital inflows via borrowing from banks)

This type of capital inflow, where it involves foreign currency operations, is subject to the same regulations as capital inflows arising from banks raising foreign currency loans abroad to finance foreign currency loans to residents (see item i) c) above). Borrowing in Euro-French francs from foreign banks is prohibited.

----

(1) In the case of resident French franc accounts, current accounts may not be remunerated. Rates of interest on customers' time deposits for up to one year and of less than 100,000 francs are regulated by the Conseil National du Crédit. Remuneration of all other deposits is without restriction. Normally these rules apply generally, but the Bank of France may suspend their application in the case of non-resident accounts, which is the position at present.

k) Capital outflows via placing liquid assets with non-resident banks

As a rule, residents are not permitted to hold accounts directly with non-resident banks, nor may they place funds in foreign money markets whether in foreign currency or domestic currency. Residents may purchase foreign currency for use in authorised transactions only through commercial banks empowered to make settlements between France and abroad ("intermédiaires agrées"), which may hold foreign exchange balances on behalf of resident non-banks. Insurance companies may hold foreign exchange balances in their own name with foreign banks, and so, with special permission, may certain non-bank financial intermediaries and certain exporting firms.

FRANCE

(situation at the end of 1980)

Type of Operation or Balance Sheet Position / Type of Regulation or Instrument	Code	I. Exchange Control (1)	II. Minimum Reserve Requirements	III. Interest Rate Control	IV. Prudential Regulations	V. Tax Regulations	VI. Other Regulations or instruments
COMMERCIAL BANKS	1.						
Liability Operations/Positions	11.						
in foreign currencies	11.1						
with non-residents	11.11						
deposits from	11.111						
banks	11.111.1						
non-banks	11.111.2						
credits and loans from	11.112						
banks	11.112.1						
non-banks	11.112.2						
fixed-interest	11.113	x					
securities							
money market paper	11.113.1						
bonds	11.113.2						
with residents	11.12						
deposits from	11.121						
banks	11.121.1						
non-banks	11.121.2	x				x	
Central Bank or Government	11.121.3						
in domestic currency	11.2						
with non-residents	11.21						
current accounts of	11.211		x				
banks	11.211.1						
non-banks	11.211.2					x	
time deposits from	11.212		x				
banks	11.212.1						
non-banks	11.212.2					x	
credits and loans from	11.213						
banks	11.213.1						
non-banks	11.213.2						
fixed-interest securities	11.214	x					
money market paper	11.214.1						
bonds	11.214.2						
Asset Operations/Positions	12.						
in foreign currencies	12.1						
with non-residents	12.11						
banks	12.111						
current accounts	12.111.1						
time deposits	12.111.2						
credits and loans	12.111.3						
non-banks	12.112						
credits and loans	12.112.1						
securities	12.113						
with residents	12.12						
deposits with banks	12.121						
credits and loans to non-banks	12.122	x					
securities	12.123						
deposits with Central bank	12.124						

(1) And similar regulations imposing quantitative controls on capital transactions with non-residents.

(Continued)   FRANCE

(situation at the end of 1980)

Type of Operation or Balance Sheet Position / Type of Regulation or Instrument	Code	I. Exchange Control (1)	II. Minimum Reserve Require-ments	III. Interest Rate Control	IV. Pruden-tial Regula-tions	V. Tax Regula-tions	VI. Other Regula-tions or instru-ments
in domestic currency	12.2						
with non-residents	12.21						
deposits with banks	12.211	x					
credits and loans to	12.212						
banks	12.212.1	x					
non-banks	12.212.2	x					
securities	12.213						
Net Positions	13.						
in foreign currencies	13.1						
vis-à-vis non-residents	13.2						
NON-BANKS	2.						
Liability Operations/Positions	21.						
credits and loans from	21.1						
non-resident banks	21.11						
in foreign currencies	21.111	x					
in domestic currency	21.112	x					
resident banks	21.12						
in foreign currencies	21.121	x					
Asset Operations/Positions	22.						
with non-resident banks	22.1	x					
in foreign currencies	22.11						
current accounts	22.111						
time deposits	22.112						
in domestic currency	22.12						
deposits	22.121						
with resident banks	22.2						
in foreign currencies	22.21	x					
current accounts	22.211						
time deposits	22.212						
FOREIGN EXCHANGE OPERATIONS/POSITIONS	3.						
Commercial Banks	31.						
spot foreign exchange dealings	31.1	x					
forward foreign exchange dealings	31.2	x					
swap transactions	31.3	x					
net foreign exchange positions	31.4	x					
Non-Banks	32.	x					
spot foreign exchange dealings	32.1	x					
forward foreign exchange dealings	32.2	x					
swap transactions	32.3	x					

(1) And similar regulations imposing quantitative controls on capital transactions with non-residents.

(situation at the end of 1980)

CODE No OF CLASSIFICATION SCHEMA	OPERATION/POSITION	REGULATION
	I. EXCHANGE CONTROL	
I/11.113	Commercial banks' issues of short-term and long-term fixed interest securities in foreign currencies to non-residents.	Subject to prior authorisation by the Ministry for the Economy.
I/11.121.2	Foreign-currency deposits from resident non-banks.	Limited to 8-day deposits under foreign exchange surrender requirements, i.e. : prohibited for maturities over 8 days.
I.11.214	Commercial banks' issues of fixed interest securities in domestic currency to non-residents.	Subject to prior authorisation by the Ministry of the Economy.
I.12.122	Commercial banks granting foreign-currency credits and loans to resident non-banks	Permitted, under general licence and without limit: foreign-currency credits for the financing of exports and imports, international trade in raw materials, the execution of contracts obtained abroad and the provision of services abroad. Also permitted under general licence: foreign currency loans for domestic use where the following conditions are met: - the rate of interest must be in keeping with normal market conditions; - borrowing proceeds must be surrendered on the foreign exchange market immediately after the loan is drawn; - the maturity must be not less than one year; - the amount of debt outstanding per borrower must not exceed the equivalent of F.Frs. 10 million.

CODE No OF CLASSIFICATION SCHEMA	OPERATION/POSITION	REGULATION
		Prior authorisation is required for all other credits and loans.
I.12.211	Commercial banks holding euro-French franc deposits with non-resident banks.	Prohibited.
I.12.212.1	Commercial banks granting credits in domestic currency to non-resident banks.	Prohibited except for occasional debit balances on correspondent accounts due to exceptional mailing delays not exceeding 10 days (mail credits).
I/12.212.2	Commercial banks granting domestic-currency credits and loans to non-resident non-banks	Generally prohibited except for certain types of credit for French exports and mortgage loans for personal use by non-residents to a maximum 50 per cent of the amount of purchase.
I/21.111) I/21.121)	Non-banks raising foreign-currency loans from resident or non-resident banks.	Permitted under general licence and without limit: foreign currency credits for the financing of imports and exports, international trade in raw materials, the execution of contracts and provision of services abroad. Also permitted under general licence: foreign-currency loans for domestic use, where the following conditions are met: - the interest rate must be in keeping with normal market conditions; - borrowing proceeds must be surrendered on the foreign exchange market immediately after the loan is drawn; - the maturity must be not less than one year; - the amount of debt outstanding per borrower must not exceed the equivalent of F.Frs. 10 million.

CODE No OF CLASSIFICATION SCHEMA	OPERATION/POSITION	REGULATION
		Prior authorisation is required for all other credits and loans.
I.21.112	Non-banks raising domestic-currency loans from non-resident banks.	Subject to prior authorisation which is not normally granted by the Minister for the Economy.
I/22.1	Non-banks building up claims on foreign banks.	Subject to prior authorisation by the Minister for the Economy. - not normally granted.
I/22.21	Non-banks' foreign-currency deposits with resident banks	Foreign currency received in the course of commercial transactions may be deposited for up to 8 days; a general obligation to surrender foreign-exchange receipts on the domestic market after 8 days.
I/31.1 I/31.2	Uncovered spot and forward foreign exchange operations by commercial banks.	Authorised subject to the rules governing foreign exchange position (see I/31.4).
I/31.3	Commercial banks' spot purchases of foreign currency from non-residents in exchange for francs, associated with a forward resale in exchange for francs (swap transaction involving a French franc loan to non-residents).	Prohibited.
I/31.4	Net spot and forward foreign exchange position.	As a general rule, commercial banks are not authorised to increase their spot and forward foreign exchange position with respect to residents and non-residents taken together globally, i.e., not each currency taken separately, on a daily basis; some long-term assets and liabilities in foreign currency fall outside the specified foreign exchange position.

CODE No OF CLASSIFICATION SCHEMA	OPERATION/POSITION	REGULATION
I/32.	Non-banks' foreign exchange operation.	Direct foreign exchange operations are prohibited; obligation to use authorised intermediary banks (intermédiaires agrées).
I/32.1	Spot foreign exchange operations by non-banks.	The holding of foreign currency assets is prohibited. Purchase of foreign currency is authorised only for settlement of international transactions and other specified operations. Obligation to surrender foreign currency receipts.
I/32.2	Forward sales or purchases of foreign currency by non-banks in exchange for domestic currency.	Forward purchases of foreign currency are authorised only for payment of imports, and for a period not exceeding 2 months. No time limit on imports of specified goods, mostly raw materials. No restriction on forward sales of foreign currency.
I/32.3	Non-banks' swap operations involving domestic currency.	Under the permitted conditions only swap transactions in which the non-bank borrows in foreign currency from a resident bank, can be undertaken.
	II. MINIMUM RESERVE REQUIREMENT	
II/11.211 11.212	Domestic currency depo- by non-residents.	Since November 1980, these are subject to a reserve requirement of 5 per cent.
	V. TAX REGULATIONS	
V/11.121.2	Foreign currency deposits by resident non-banks.	Interest paid on these accounts is subject to a 40% withholding tax (unless a depositor being an individual opts for the progressive income tax).

CODE No OF CLASSIFICATION SCHEMA	OPERATION/POSITION	REGULATION
V/11.211.2 V/11.212.2	Balances on current account and Time-deposits in domestic currency by non-resident non-banks.	Interest payable on these accounts is subject to a 40% withholding tax.

V. PRINCIPAL SOURCES OF LEGAL AND
REGULATORY PROVISIONS

Exchange Controls (and similar regulations imposing quantitative
limitations on capital operations with non-residents)

Decree No. 67-78 of 27th January, 1967 specifying the
modalities of application of the Act No. 66-1008 of 28th
December, 1966 concerning the external financial relations.

Decree No. 68-1021 of 24th November, 1968 regulating the
external financial relations.

Order of 9th August, 1973 concerning the specification of
certain modalities of application of the Decree No. 68-1021
of 24th November, 1968 regulating the external financial
relations.

(and Circular of 9th August, 1973)

Note: Detailed rules of application are issued by:

- the Directorate of Treasury in the form of notes;
- the Banque de France in various forms such as letters and
  notes;
- the Directorate General of Customs and Indirect Taxes in
  the form of circulars and notes published in the Bulletin
  Officiel des Douanes.

Minimum Reserve Requirements

Decree of 9th January, 1967/23rd February, 1971 concerning
the system of mandatory reserves.

Decision of a general character No. 71-01 of 10th January,
1966/26th February, 1971 of the National Credit Council
concerning the system of mandatory reserves.

Note: Detailed rules of application are issued by the Banque de
France in the form of "instructions" (especially Instruction
No. 89 of 26th February, 1971).

Tax Regulations

General Tax Code (articles 124 A and 125 A, Annex III,
Section 41 duodecies c).

GERMANY

I. INTRODUCTION

i) Main characteristics of the regulatory system

Germany has been a substantial source of net
capital exports in the seventies, as corresponds to the
country's basic position as a net exporter of goods and
services and which is in line with policy intentions.   Owing
to an efficient financial system which, moreover, operates traditionally under a regime of freedom of capital movements, substantial
amounts of exported capital have been made available in long-term
forms such as foreign bond issues and long-term bank loans. Moreover,
the banking system plays an important role as an intermediary for the
placement of DM funds; by contrast, foreign-currency business with
non-residents has remained less important than in a number of other,
including smaller, countries as the authorities have abstained from
favouring the development of euro-currency markets within their own
territory.

Since the early sixties, given the attraction of the Deutsche
Mark as an investment currency resulting from persistently large
current account surpluses, the authorities have several times had to
cope with destabilising capital inflows which assumed substantial
dimensions when expectations of a revaluation of the currency became
widespread.   Under these circumstances the authorities, whilst maintaining full freedom for all types of capital exports, have repeatedly
taken measures to ward off large waves of capital inflows or to neu-
tralise their expansionary effects on domestic bank and non-bank
liquidity which threatened domestic monetary stability, notably
during periods of domestic overheating.

The principal weapons for keeping bank liquidity under control
have been minimum-reserve requirements on both outstanding amounts of,
and increases in, non-resident and resident deposits and the virtual
prohibition of interest payments on non-resident bank deposits whether
denominated in DM or foreign currencies. Additional instruments designed to counteract capital inflows into the non-bank sector and
the domestic securities markets were introduced under the exceptional
circumstances of the early seventies: first, the so-called "Bardepot"

47

system of minimum-reserve requirements on credits raised abroad by domestic non-banks and on long-term borrowing of financial institutions which were not subject to the traditional reserve requirements; second, direct administrative controls on non-bank borrowing abroad; third, straight-forward prohibition of non-resident purchases of domestic securities. Recourse to these latter measures was had only with great reluctance and for a relatively short period as the authorities have traditionally adhered to the principle of freedom of international capital movements.

During certain periods of the late 1950's, the 1960's and the early 1970's, special central bank swap facilities for encouraging the export or re-export of short-term banking funds also belonged to the arsenal of weapons for fighting undesirable capital inflows; however, as the banks tended to make increasing use of these facilities for benefitting from "merry-go-round" transactions i.e. deliberate capital import and re-export operations, the use of this technique was abandoned in the early seventies. From 1979 onwards, under different circumstances foreign-exchange swap transactions and repurchase agreements were effected in both directions as a fine-tuning and short-term operation in order to influence both liquidity and to smooth out exchange rate fluctuations.

A new measure affecting the individual banks' foreign-exchange position and practically eliminating the banks' scope for incurring open positions both in the spot and forward exchange markets was introduced in October 1974 in the wake of the Herstatt affair. However, this measure was primarily aimed at limiting the banks' risks in foreign-exchange transactions rather than influencing their external positions in a monetary policy context.

Today (1), only relatively moderate restrictions on, and obstacles to, some types of capital imports are still in force: first, non-resident investments in domestic money-market paper or relatively short-term investments in the security markets are subject to approval, which is not normally granted; and second, minimum-reserve requirements which apply to non-resident and resident deposits with a maturity of less than four years, whether denominated in domestic or foreign currencies, continue to provide no incentive for banks in Germany to raise short-term funds abroad and to participate in the international syndication of medium-term foreign-currency credits. Exempted from minimum-reserve requirements are only non-resident foreign-currency deposits which serve to finance specific and narrowly defined interest-rate arbitrage operations with other financial centres or imports of goods and services by resident firms.

---

(1) The situation described in terms of regulations is, for all country notes contained in this publication, the one prevailing at end of 1980.

The present regulatory setting does not, however, prevent German banks from engaging actively in operations with other euro-market centres where they generally tend to maintain net supplier positions both in foreign currencies and in Deutsche Mark; in addition, German banks have become important suppliers of funds via traditional foreign bank lending (in domestic currency) to non-bank borrowers abroad. German non-banking firms, on the other hand, even in the absence of tight domestic credit conditions, have tended to maintain net borrower positions vis-à-vis the Euro-DM market which is explained by the fact that Euro-DM loans generally offer better terms to borrowers than domestic DM loans, mainly because foreign lenders are not subject to the same minimum-reserve requirements as banks located in Germany. In this way, the regulatory system in Germany favours the expansion of Euro-DM transactions. Incentives in this direction were even stronger in the past when the remuneration of non-resident DM deposits with banks in Germany was practically prohibited and when minimum reserve ratios stood much higher than at present.

ii)   Selected data on international banking operations

Germany is the fourth most important international financial centre after the United Kingdom, the United States and France, mainly because of substantial intermediation of long-term foreign DM funds and net exports of domestic-currency funds; however, as a euro-market centre Germany ranks only eighth before Sweden amongst the twelve European countries reporting to the Bank for International Settlements at the end of 1978. On the other hand, within Europe the German banking system is at present the most important lender of domestic currencies and after the Swiss and French banking systems the third largest net capital exporter amongst all European countries' banking systems.

Between end-1973 and end-1978, external assets and liabilities in domestic and foreign currencies of banks located in Germany rose from US$ 14.8 billion to US$ 61.1 billion and from US$ 15.7 billion to US$ 59.1 billion, respectively, with their market share in international banking business of the European (1) countries reporting to the Bank for International Settlements rising from 7.1 per cent to

(1) The market share is measured as a percentage of total external foreign-currency liabilities of banks of the European countries (counting Belgium and Luxembourg separately) reporting to the Bank for International Settlements.

10.0 per cent on the asset side and from 7.0 per cent to equally
10.0 per cent on the liabilities side. Germany's position as a
euro-market centre proper remained roughly stable on a relatively
low level with its share in total external foreign-currency deposits
increasing from 3.5 per cent to 3.8 per cent in the same period.

Despite Germany's chronic balance-of-payments
surpluses until the end of the seventies, only in recent
years has the German banking system turned from a net

capital importer to a net capital exporter position, which at the
end of 1978 amounted to US$ 2 billion as compared with a net liability
position of US$ 0.9 billion prevailing at the end of 1973. The bulk
of the turn-round in the net external position took place in the domestic-currency sector. However, at the end of 1978, the net external
position in domestic-currency was practically balanced, while the net
external position in foreign currencies moved from near-equilibrium
to a moderate net asset position of US$ 2 billion.

Foreign business of banks in Germany has expanded more rapidly
in recent years than domestic business with the shares of foreign
assets and liabilities in balance-sheet totals rising from 6.7 per
cent to 9.7 per cent and from 4.9 per cent to 7.5 per cent, respectively, between end-1973 and end-1978 (1).

The Deutsche Mark is the second most important euro-currency
after the US dollar and before the Swiss franc with a market share
of roughly 19 per cent at the end of 1978. It is interesting to
note that banks in centres outside Germany are more important as
international borrowers and lenders of DM funds than the banking
system in Germany, with DM assets held by banks outside Germany (2)

---

(1) The ratios mentioned are derived from data published in the
    IMF International Financial Statistics on Deposit Money Banks
    which, inter alia, include external long-term claims of the
    Kreditanstalt für Wiederaufbau and are, therefore, not fully
    comparable with BIS data on banks' external positions; it
    should be noted that the German banking system, according to
    the concepts used in IMF International Financial Statistics,
    is more widely defined than that of other countries and that,
    therefore, the share of international business of German com-
    mercial banks proper is considerably understated.

(2) Including DM assets held with banks and non-banks located in
    Germany.

amounting at the end of 1978 to the equivalent of US$ 97.4 billion
as compared with external DM claims of banks in Germany of the equivalent of US$ 40.3 billion; at the same time, Euro-DM deposits
amounted to the equivalent of US$ 93.1 billion as compared with
external DM liabilities of banks in Germany of the equivalent of
US$ 40.2 billion. The most important centres for Euro-DM funds are
located in Luxembourg and London.

The structure of Euro-DM liabilities of banks in the European
countries reporting to the BIS is characterized by a relatively low
share of private non-bank deposits (6.5 per cent), whereas holdings
by official monetary institutions are relatively important (17.9 per
cent). The remaining three quarters were liabilities vis-à-vis other
non-resident banks. The structure of Euro-DM assets, however, shows
a large share of credits extended to private non-banks (25.4 per cent),
of which German non-banks play a dominant role (16.1 per cent of total
Euro-DM assets).

The total share of Euro-DM assets held with German residents
was 33.6 per cent end of 1978, compared with 21.4 per cent end of
1973. The corresponding share of Euro-DM liabilities vis-à-vis
German residents (mostly banks) remained stable at roughly 12 per
cent, though it had been a few percentage points higher a few years
earlier.

II. ANALYSIS OF REGULATIONS BY MAIN TYPES
OF CAPITAL MOVEMENTS

(situation at the end of 1980)

i)   Commercial banks' foreign-currency operations

a) External foreign-currency borrowing for relending abroad

Apart from the nearly equal treatment of domestic and foreign
deposits by minimum reserve requirements, there are at present no
obstacles - either in the form of exchange controls, interest controls,
or taxes - to commercial banks taking foreign-currency deposits or
raising foreign-currency credits abroad for re-employing these funds
in various forms (money market investments, loans and credits,
securities) abroad (or domestically).

Notwithstanding certain narrowly circumscribed exceptions,
foreign-currency (as well as domestic-currency) liabilities to non-
resident banks and non-banks with maturities up to less than four

years are subject to minimum-reserve requirements. Incremental
reserve requirements on liabilities to non-residents applying to
the growth of such liabilities above specified levels, at times
were raised up to a ratio of 100 per cent. Since 1969, when the
Bundesbank Act was revised, minimum-reserve ratios for external
liabilities may be raised up to 100 per cent.

There are two main types of exemptions from the obligation to
maintain minimum reserves against non-resident liabilities which are
relevant to euro-market operations. In their present form they came
into effect on 20th June, 1975 when the conditions under which these
exemptions were granted were redefined in more restrictive terms.
Another minor change took place in mid-1978. Basically, these
exceptions are as follows:

1) The first exemption applies to foreign-currency funds
   raised abroad for relending abroad, on condition that
   the claim is in the same currency and has the same
   maturity as the liability. Typical transactions falling
   under this heading are international interbank market
   operations for interest-rate arbitrage purposes.

   Not exempt from reserve requirements are the following
   liability items or operations: sight liabilities or
   liabilities with an agreed period of notice and, since
   the change in regulations of June 1975, short-term funds
   raised abroad on a roll-over basis for the financing of
   medium- or long-term euro-credits to non-banks, even if
   the depositor remains the same.

2) The second exemption relates to the raising of foreign-
   and domestic-currency credits on behalf of customers for
   import financing. The identity of the currency borrowed
   and lent, congruity of maturities and the non-prolongation
   requirement again are the main requirements for this
   exemption.

There was an additional obstacle insofar as the remuneration
of external foreign-currency (and domestic-currency) deposits in a
narrow sense was subject to authorisation which was not normally
granted. However, this virtual prohibition of interest payment did
not apply to loans and credits raised abroad by German banks on their
own initiative. The ban on remuneration of external deposits was
lifted in September 1975.

b) Capital inflows via inward switching

Commercial banks are free to switch foreign-currency assets into domestic currency. However, as explained in section i) a) above, external liabilities of less than four years in foreign currencies (and domestic currency) are subject to minimum-reserve requirements just like liabilities to resident non-banks, though reserve ratios may be different. Relatively high incremental reserve ratios may also be applied which provide a strong disincentive for banks to raise external foreign-currency deposits for inward switching purposes.

External foreign-currency (and domestic-currency) liabilities with maturities of four years and longer, whether used for domestic lending in domestic or foreign currencies (or even for relending abroad), are no longer subject to any restrictions. In the period from March 1972 to August 1974, this type of capital inflow was impaired by a special cash deposit scheme (Bardepot).

Since October 1974, there is limited scope for uncovered inward switching. Under a new rule (the so-called Principle Ia), introduced in October 1974 within the framework of prudential regulation, as established by the Federal Banking Supervisory Office in agreement with the Deutsche Bundesbank, open positions of individual banks must not exceed a specified percentage of liable capital including reserves.(1)

c) Capital inflows via the use of foreign-currency funds raised abroad for granting foreign-currency loans to resident non-banks

This type of capital inflow is impaired by minimum reserve requirements applying to external foreign-currency liabilities up to less than four years, except if matched by foreign-currency lending to the banks' customers for import financing on specified conditions (see section i) a) above). In addition, foreign-currency credits and loans to resident non-banks with maturities of more than one year are subject to special authorisation by the Bundesbank which is not normally granted in order to avoid foreign-currency indexation. However, operations of this kind with maturities of up to one year and foreign-currency deposits with resident banks are generally authorised.

(1)   This rule was completed as from 1st February by including gold, silver and platinum metals. This completion was indicated by heavy price movements in the market for precious metals.

d) Capital outflows via outward switching

There are no limitations on capital outflows via banks switching domestic currency into foreign-currency assets, though since the introduction of "Principle 1a" (see section i) b) above) such outflows can practically take place only on a covered basis.

In the late fifties and sixties, the Bundesbank at certain times of excessive capital inflows encourage such outward switching by providing forward cover at preferential swap rates. In September 1969, it discontinued its swap operations when it realised that the credit policy objective of the swap operations, namely to rechannel speculative foreign exchange inflows into foreign money markets, was being undermined by "roundabout" transactions by means of which the banks were able, without using their own funds, to secure a profit corresponding roughly to the difference between the swap rate of the market and that of the Bundesbank. The same experience reoccurred on 1st April, 1971 when swap operations were reintroduced; they had to be discontinued the following day.

e) Capital outflows via financing external foreign-currency assets with foreign-currency deposits from resident non-banks

This type of capital outflow, while not impeded directly, is affected by minimum reserve requirements to which resident deposits up to less than four years are subject. Banks are not willing to offer euro-market rates on such deposits because of the cost effects of minimum reserves. For this and other reasons such as the possibility of a resident non-bank maintaining deposits abroad or concluding swap transactions with domestic banks are relatively unimportant.

ii) Commercial banks' domestic-currency operations with non-residents

f) Domestic-currency liabilities to non-residents

Domestic-currency liabilities to non-resident banks and non-banks with maturities of up to less than four years are subject to the same minimum reserve requirements as foreign-currency liabilities to non-residents (see section i) a) above).

Since September 1975, interest rates paid on non-resident deposits can be the same as those offered to residents. Before that date, the payment of interest on non-resident deposits was practically prohibited (see section i) a) above). The imposition of minimum reserve requirements provides an incentive for German banks to channel part of their domestic-currency deposit and lending business with non-residents through foreign subsidiaries and branches, with a view to avoiding the cost effects of minimum reserves on lending margins.

In early 1980, in view of large-scale DM borrowings of German banks in the form of borrowers' notes of indentedness in the years before and with the purpose of restraining the use of the D-Mark as international reserve currency, voluntary understanding was reached with German banks limiting those borrowings to remaining maturities of five years or more. Subsequently, in concurrence with comparable legal restrictions for non-residents to acquire domestic money market paper and similar bonds, and in view of the emerging deficit in the current account of the German balance of payments, the maturity barrier of five years was lowered in two steps to one year.

g) Placing domestic-currency funds with foreign banks

There are no legal obstacles to this type of capital outflow. (see also (ii) g)).

h) Domestic-currency credits and loans to non-resident non-banks

There are no legal restrictions on this type of capital outflow; however, because of the cost effects of minimum reserves on domestic-currency liabilities, banks in Germany are at a disadvantage in granting DM loans to non-resident non-bank borrowers as compared with banks abroad, including foreign subsidiaries and branches of German banks, granting euro-DM loans to such borrowers. In December 1980 banks in Germany were requested by the Deutsche Bundesbank to refrain voluntarily and for a limited period (end of March 1981) from DM-lending to non-residents on a long-term basis (four years and more) if the lending is not related to the financing of German exports and if the lending is more than DM 10 million on an individual basis.

Memorandum Item:

Transactions with non-residents in fixed-interest securities in domestic currency

Fixed-interest securities in domestic and foreign currencies issued by non-residents can be freely bought by residents and resold by them to non-residents. The same applies to fixed-interest securities issued by residents, though with one exception as regards selling them to non-residents. Up to March 1980 the acquisition by non-residents against payment from residents of money market paper in domestic currency, of bonds which mature as a whole or whose last redemption payment falls due within four years, and of bonds with repurchase obligations at a fixed price falling due within four years was still subject to authorisation by the Bundesbank. Since then the maturity barrier of four years has been lowered in two steps to one year (see also (ii) f). The payment to non-residents on the domestic market is generally subject to a with-holding tax of 25 per cent, which has been in force since March 1965.

iii) <u>Non-banking borrowing and lending operations with non-resident banks</u>

j) <u>Capital inflows via borrowing from non-resident banks</u>

There are no restrictions on this type of capital inflow whether in domestic currency or foreign currencies. In the period March 1972 to August 1974, such operations were impaired by a special cash deposit scheme (Bardepot) under which a specified percentage of imported amounts had to be deposited with the Bundesbank in a non-interest bearing account. From February 1973 to January 1974, this scheme was supplemented by a ruling that all loans from abroad to residents had to be authorised.

k) <u>Capital outflows via placing liquid assets with non-resident banks</u>

Resident non-banks are entirely free to open accounts with foreign banks and to place liquid funds on national foreign money markets and the euro-market, including the euro-DM market.

III. SUMMARY VIEW OF REGULATIONS AND INSTRUMENTS AFFECTING INTERNATIONAL
BANKING OPERATIONS OF BANKS AND NON-BANKS IN

GERMANY

(situation at the end of 1980)

Type of Operation or Balance Sheet Position / Type of Regulation or Instrument	Code	I. Exchange Control (1)	II. Minimum Reserve Requirements	III. Interest Rate Control	IV. Prudential Regulations	V. Tax Regulations	VI. Other Regulations or instruments
COMMERCIAL BANKS	1.						
Liability Operations/Positions	11.						
in foreign currencies	11.1						
with non-residents	11.11						
deposits from	11.111		x				x
banks	11.111.1						
non-banks	11.111.2						
credits and loans from	11.112		x				x
banks	11.112.1						
non-banks	11.112.2						
fixed-interest	11.113	x					
securities							
money market paper	11.113.1						
bonds	11.113.2					x	
with residents	11.12						
deposits from	11.121						
banks	11.121.1						
non-banks	11.121.2						
Central Bank or Government	11.121.3						
in domestic currency	11.2						
with non-residents	11.21						
current accounts of	11.211		x				
banks	11.211.1						
non-banks	11.211.2						
time deposits from	11.212		x				x
banks	11.212.1						
non-banks	11.212.2						
credits and loans from	11.213		x				x
banks	11.213.1						
non-banks	11.213.2						
fixed-interest securities	11.214	x					
money market paper	11.214.1						
bonds	11.214.2					x	
Asset Operations/Positions	12.						
in foreign currencies	12.1						
with non-residents	12.11						x
banks	12.111						
current accounts	12.111.1						
time deposits	12.111.2						
credits and loans	12.111.3						
non-banks	12.112						
credits and loans	12.112.1						
securities	12.113	x					
with residents	12.12						
deposits with banks	12.121						
credits and loans to non-banks	12.122	x					
securities	12.123						
deposits with Central bank	12.124						

(1) And similar regulations imposing quantitative controls on capital transactions with non-residents.

<u>GERMANY</u>

(situation at the end of 1980)

Type of Operation or Balance Sheet Position / Type of Regulation or Instrument	Code	I. Exchange Control (1)	II. Minimum Reserve Requirements	III. Interest Rate Control	IV. Prudential Regulations	V. Tax Regulations	VI. Other Regulations or instruments
in domestic currency	12.2						
with non-residents	12.21						x
deposits with banks	12.211						
credits and loans to	12.212						
banks	12.212.1						
non-banks	12.212.2						
securities	12.213	x					
Net Positions	13.						
in foreign currencies	13.1		x		x		
vis-à-vis non-residents	13.2						
NON-BANKS	2.						
Liability Operations/ Positions	21.						
credits and loans from	21.1						
non-resident banks	21.11						
in foreign currencies	21.111						
in domestic currency	21.112						
resident banks	21.12						
in foreign currencies	21.121	x					
Asset Operations/Positions	22.						
with non-resident banks	22.1						
in foreign currencies	22.11						
current accounts	22.111						
time deposits	22.112						
in domestic currency	22.12						
deposits	22.121						
with resident banks	22.2						
in foreign currencies	22.21						
current accounts	22.211						
time deposits	22.212						
FOREIGN EXCHANGE OPERATIONS/ POSITIONS	3.						
Commercial Banks	31.						
spot foreign exchange dealings	31.1						
forward foreign exchange dealings	31.2						
swap transactions	31.3						
net foreign exchange positions	31.4				x		
Non-Banks	32.						
spot foreign exchange dealings	32.1						
forward foreign exchange dealings	32.2						
swap transactions	32.3						

(1) And similar regulations imposing quantitative controls on capital transactions with non-residents.

IV. LISTING OF REGULATIONS BY CATEGORIES AND BY OPERATIONS ON BALANCE SHEET POSITIONS

(situation at the end of 1980)

CODE No OF CLASSIFICATION SCHEMA	OPERATION/POSITION	REGULATION

I. EXCHANGE CONTROL

I/11.113) I/11.214) I/12.113) I/12.213)	Selling to non-residents of fixed-interest securities in domestic and foreign currencies issued by residents.	Subject to authorisation in the sale to non-residents of resident-issued money market paper in domestic currency and bonds which mature as a whole or whose last redemption payment falls due within one year and the sale of bonds with repurchase obligation at a fixed price falling due within one year.
I/12.122	Commercial banks granting) foreign-currency credits and) loans to resident non-banks.)	Subject to special authorisation by the Bundesbank if maturities exceed one year. Foreign-currency credits and loans to resident non-banks with maturities of one year and less and foreign-currency deposits with resident banks are allowed under general authorisation.
I/21/121	Resident non-banks borrowing) foreign-currency credit and) loans from resident banks.)	

II. MINIMUM RESERVE REQUIREMENTS

II/11.111) II/11.112) II/13.1)	Commercial banks taking from) non-resident banks and non-) banks deposits or loans in) foreign currencies which are) not matched by loans exten-) ded for import financing or) by specified foreign-) currency assets under nar-) rowly defined conditions:) (for details see Section II))	Maturities up to less than four years are subject to minimum-reserve requirements in the form of non-interest bearing central bank balances.
	Commercial banks taking de-) posits in foreign currency) from resident non-banks,) including the public sector,) and from banks not subject) to reserve requirements.))	From 1st August, 1975 to end-1977, reserve ratios on liabilities to non-residents were same as those on liabilities to residents. This holds again since 1st June, 1978. The following ratios on outstanding amounts of

II. MINIMUM RESERVE REQUIREMENTS
(continued)

		liabilities are in effect since 1st **September** 1980
		12.1 per cent on sight deposits
		8.5 per cent on time deposits
		5.4 per cent on savings deposits.
II/11.211 II/11.212 II/11.213	Commercial banks taking from non-resident banks and non-banks deposits and loans in domestic currency which are not matched by loans extended for import financing.	

IV. PRUDENTIAL REGULATIONS

IV/13.1) IV/31.4)	Each **bank's** open exchange position in foreign currencies, i.e. the difference between all foreign exchange credit and debt positions (excluding notes and coins but including fixed-interest securities and forward positions).(1)	Limitation to 30 per cent of liable funds at the close of business each day. In calculating the difference, only credit and debt positions in the same currency can be netted against each other. Furthermore, the sum of negative and positive net positions (disregarding the signs) in all currencies due within any calendar month and between January **and** June or between July and December of any **year** is limited to 40 per cent of liable funds, also on day-to-day basis.

V. TAX REGULATIONS

V/11.113.2) V/11.214.2)	Interest payments to non-residents on securities issued by residents on the domestic market.	Interest payments on all fixed-interest securities issued by residents are generally subject to a withholding tax of 25 per cent, provided that the interest is being paid in form of a coupon, that more than one bond has been issued in connection with the loans or that the claim has been entered into a public debt register.

---

(1)   As from 1st February, 1980, gold, silver and platinum metals were also included.

CODE NO. OF CLASSIFICATION SCHEMA	OPERATION/POSITION	REGULATION

VI. OTHER REGULATIONS OR INSTRUMENTS

VI/11.111) VI/11.112) VI/11.212) VI/11.213)	Deposits and credits and loans from non-residents in domestic and foreign currencies.	On a voluntary basis German banks have been asked to refrain from borrowings in the form of borrowers' notes of indebtedness with a maturity of less than one year.
VI/12.11) VI/12.21)	Lending abroad in domestic and foreign currencies	On a voluntary basis German banks have been asked to refrain temporarily from long-term lending with a maturity of more than four years if the lending is not related to the financing of German exports and if the lending is more than DM 10 million on an individual basis.

V. PRINCIPAL SOURCES OF LEGAL AND
REGULATORY PROVISIONS

Exchange Controls (and similar regulations imposing quantitative limitations on capital operations with non-residents)

> Foreign Trade and Payments Act of 28th April, 1961, as amended

> Foreign Trade and Payments Order of 22nd August, 1961, as amended

Note: Detailed rules of application are introduced in the form of orders amending the Foreign Trade and Payments Order of 22nd August, 1961 issued by the Federal Government and notices issued by the Deutsche Bundesbank

> Currency Act of June 1948 (Article 3) (applying only to Code No. 12.12 of Section III of the present country note, i.e. foreign-currency denominated credits granted by resident banks to resident non-banks)

> The Foreign Trade and Payments Act and the Foreign Trade and Payments Order do not apply to trade and payments between the Federal Republic of Germany and West Berlin on the one hand and the German Democratic Republic and East Berlin on the other. Such trade and payments are subject to special laws and regulations

Minimum-Reserve Requirements

> Deutsche Bundesbank Act of 26th July, 1957 (Paragraph 16)

> Minimum Reserve Order of 11th November, 1968, as amended

Prudential Regulations

> Banking Act of 15th July, 1961, as amended on May 3, 1976

> Announcement No. 1/62 of 8th March, 1962 and No. 1/69 of 20th January, 1969 of the Federal Banking Supervisory Office on the principles concerning the capital and liquidity of banks

> Amendment of 30th August, 1974 to the principles concerning the capital and liquidity of banks (introduction of Principle 1a concerning the foreign-exchange position of individual banks: see Code No. 13.1 and 31.4 of Section III of the present country note)

Tax Regulations

> "Coupon Tax Act", of 27th March, 1965 to amend and supplement the Income-Tax Act and Capital-transaction-tax Act

THE NETHERLANDS

I. INTRODUCTION

i)   Main purposes of the regulatory system

For most of the past decade, the Netherlands economy has been
a source of net capital exports, conforming to the structural policy
to free a part of domestic resources for the benefit of the developing
world. Its financial system has relatively close links with foreign
financial markets and plays a significant role in the international
intermediation of funds.

Nevertheless, the authorities aim to exercise effective control
over operations which could most directly interfere with orderly conditions in the domestic capital markets, lead to - from a monetary
policy point of view - undesirable capital inflows, or enhance the
international role of the guilder as a reserve asset. Subject to such
safeguards, the export of capital is basically free, as is capital
import except for mainly short- and medium-term types constituting
a practicable substitute for domestic bank credit (which at present is
subject to restriction). The regulatory instruments are utilised in a
flexible manner.

Authorised banks enjoy a high degree of freedom in carrying out
international intermediation operations (1). Corresponding lending and
borrowing operations are free; certain longer-term lending operations
such as the participation in internationally syndicated euro-credits
are permitted under general authorisation. There are no obstacles in
the form of reserve requirements or tax provisions. Repatriation of
net foreign assets is free, e.g. under special swap facilities provided by the Netherlands Bank, a technique which assures the re-export
of banking funds after temporary domestic liquidity needs have been met.

Non-banks are not allowed to take up financial credits abroad
above an individual ceiling of Fl. 500,000 a year, nor to issue bonds

---

(1) I.e. borrowing foreign-currency funds abroad for relending to non-
    residents.

abroad - unless authorised (1) - in order to insulate the financial
system as far as feasible from unwanted capital inflows initiated by
residents. Non-residents remain free to invest in Dutch real or
financial assets (e.g. through direct investments and stock exchange
investments, respectively). In the past, however, from 1972 to 1975,
when foreign demand for guilders tended to push the exchange rate up
too high and excessive inflows of capital were also undesirable from a
domestic monetary control point of view, the acquisition of guilder
deposits by non-residents was counteracted both by the prohibition of
interest payments on sight deposits and by preventing domestic banks
from accepting non-resident time deposits.

From 1964 up to June 1979, domestic banks were prohibited from
acting as channels for net imports of capital insofar as they were not
allowed to maintain a net spot external liability position in excess
of Fl. 5 million per bank. Subsequently, the permitted maximum net
external liability positions were differentiated by bringing them into
proportion with the amount of each bank's gross foreign business as
measured by the gross external asset position at the end of 1978 and
progressively increased in view of the erosion of the banks' total net
foreign asset position as a consequence of balance-of-payments developments. Towards the end of January 1980, the regulation was terminated.

In conformity with the structural balance-of-payments policy,
capital exports are free as a general rule, but with two limitations.
First, public issues and private placements by non-residents on the
Dutch capital market are regulated through a queue system; in the
private placement sector the amounts and maturities of loans to non-
residents are, moreover, subject to conditions which may be adjusted to
the prevailing capital market situation. Second, the purchase by
residents of unlisted euro-guilder securities (e.g. notes) issued by
non-residents is not permitted (2). The purpose of these exceptions
to the general rule is not to limit capital exports as such, but to
safeguard orderly conditions in the domestic capital market and to help
regulate the total amount of foreign euro-guilder securities outstanding in the offshore market.

On the other hand, the authorities do not wish, in the absence
of co-ordinated international regulation of the euro-currency markets,
to put the Dutch banking system at a competitive disadvantage. So the

_____

(1) At present, permission for the transfer of loan proceeds into the
    country is given only if they are from long-term loans that meet
    specified conditions regarding minimum maturities and interest rate
    adjustment.
(2) Domestic banks, in their function as market makers, are allowed to
    buy unlisted guilder securities (e.g. notes) issued by non-residents
    on condition that they are resold to non-residents.

banks are free to supply funds in domestic and foreign currency to
foreign banks and other non-residents and they may thus contribute to
the growth of the euro-guilder and other euro-currency markets.

ii)   Selected data on international banking operations

        The Netherlands position as a centre for international banking
activity is of about the same importance as that of Switzerland, not
counting the latter's role as an intermediary of non-resident fiduciary
funds. Foreign-currency business is much more important than activity
in domestic currency though there has been a noticeable expansion in
external guilder-denominated bank assets and liabilities in recent
years.

        In the period between the end of 1973 and 1979, external bank
assets and liabilities rose from US $ 10.3 billion to US $55.9 billion and from US $ 10.8 billion to US $55.5 billion, respectively,
which meant an increase in the market share in international banking
business of the European countries reporting to the Bank for International Settlements from 4.9 per cent to 7.2 per cent on both the
asset and liability side. Part of the strengthening of the Netherlands
position in international banking activity took place in the euro-
market sector where its market share rose from 5.0 per cent to 6.7 per
cent in the same period (1).

        In line with balance-of-payments trends in recent years, the
Netherlands banking system has changed its net external position from
near-equilibrium at the end of 1973 to a net exporter position of
around $ 3 billion (essentially in foreign currencies) at its peak
in early 1977, and subsequently back to near-equilibrium at the end
of 1979.

        The expansion of international banking activity in the
Netherlands is also reflected in the banking system's balance sheets
where, between end-1973 and end-1979, the share of foreign business
rose from 30 per cent to 34 per cent on the asset side and from 27 per
cent to 33½ per cent on the liabilities side (2).

        As a euro-currency the Dutch guilder plays about the same rela-
tively small role as the pound sterling and the French franc; banks

---

(1) The market share is measured as a percentage of total external
    foreign-currency liabilities of banks of the European coun-
    tries (counting Belgium and Luxembourg separately) reporting to the
    Bank for International Settlements.
(2) The ratios mentioned are derived from data published in IMF Inter-
    national Financial Statistics on Deposit Money Banks which exclude
    domestic interbank deposits.

in the Netherlands are free to supply domestic currency funds to the euro-market. At the end of 1978, euro-guilder deposits amounted to the equivalent of US $ 7.4 billion, i.e. roughly 1.5 per cent of total euro-currency deposits of banks in the European countries reporting to the Bank for International Settlements. Guilder assets and liabilities of banks outside the Netherlands (1) are slightly less important than foreign guilder assets and liabilities of banks in the Netherlands. The main centres for euro-guilder deposit business are located in the United Kingdom, Belgium, Luxembourg and France.

II. ANALYSIS OF REGULATIONS BY MAIN TYPES OF CAPITAL MOVEMENTS

(situation at the end of 1980)

i) Commercial banks' foreign-currency operations

a) External foreign-currency borrowing for relending abroad

Authorised banks enjoy a high degree of freedom in carrying out foreign-currency borrowing and lending business with non-resident banks and non-banks. There are no obstacles in the form of minimum reserve requirements, interest-rate controls or withholding taxes on interest payment on foreign-currency liabilities. Borrowing in the form of foreign currency bonds and notes is subject to individual licence which, however, is normally granted. Interbank deposit operations in foreign currencies and the taking of foreign-currency deposits from non-resident non-banks are free. Longer-term lending to non-resident non-banks (in excess of Fl. 10 million per year by each individual bank to an individual foreign debtor), including the participation in internationally syndicated medium-term euro-currency loans, is subject to licence but is at present freely permitted under general authorisation.

b) Capital inflows via inward switching

Authorised banks are free under general licence to switch foreign-currency assets into domestic currency on a covered basis. The Netherlands Bank may facilitate inward switching of foreign-currency assets by providing swap facilities which are mainly used for achieving a temporary easing of the domestic money market. There is only limited scope for uncovered inward switching. The authorised banks are obliged to comply with requests from the Netherlands Bank - on the basis of extensive and frequent information supplied by them - to reduce or eliminate uncovered positions in any individual foreign currency (i.e. to balance their spot and their forward positions in such a currency, vis-à-vis residents and non-residents taken together) if the Bank considers such open positions too large or protracted.

(1) See footnote 1.to Table 1 of Annex II.

c) Capital inflows via the use of foreign-currency funds raised abroad for granting foreign-currency loans to resident non-banks

In practice, the demand for such loans has been small; no restrictive regulations on this type of capital inflows are presently enforced.

d) Capital outflows via outward switching

There are at present no limitations on capital outflows via banks switching domestic currency into foreign-currency assets on a covered basis. There is only very limited scope for uncovered outward switching, for the same reason as set out in section i) b) above.

e) Capital outflows via financing external foreign-currency assets with foreign-currency deposits from resident bon-banks

Under exchange-control regulations, resident banks and non-banks are free to hold foreign-currency deposits with domestic banks. Thus, there is no quantitative control over this type of capital outflow.

ii)   Commercial banks' domestic-currency operations with non-residents

f) Domestic-currency liabilities to non-residents

There are at present no obstacles for banks to incur guilder liabilities to non-residents. The taking of guilder deposits from non-residents is free. Active guilder borrowing abroad in the form of bond and note issues is subject to individual licence which, however, is normally granted. Only the sale of guilder money market paper (e.g. bankers' acceptances), and the assignment of guilder claims on residents, to non-residents is prohibited.

From March 1972 to end-1975 the taking of guilder deposits from non-residents was discouraged in two ways: first, by prohibiting the remuneration of sight deposits; and second, by not allowing banks to accept guilder time deposits (apart from certain exemptions applying to savings accounts of private individuals).

g) Placing domestic-currency funds with foreign banks

Banks are allowed to place guilder balances with foreign banks and thereby supply funds to the euro-guilder market.

h) Domestic-currency credits and loans to non-residents non-banks

Guilder bank credits and loans to non-resident non-banks of maturities of up to twelve months, are free. Longer-term credits and loans are free up to Fl. 10 million per year per foreign debtor; additional amounts may be lent under general authorisation.

iii) Non-bank borrowing and lending operations with non-resident banks

   j) Capital inflows via borrowing from non-resident banks

     Foreign bank credits or loans (apart from mortgage loans on real
estate situated abroad), whether in foreign or domestic currency, in
excess of Fl. 500,000 a year per borrower, are subject to individual
licence by the Netherlands Bank. Commercial credits are permitted if
they are directly connected with specific commercial transactions with
non-residents and not of a longer duration than the customary term in
the business concerned. As to financial credits, any transfer of loan
proceeds into the country is permitted only if they are from long-term
loans that meet specified conditions regarding minimum maturities and
interest /either (1) last repayment of principal after at least ten
years, average maturity at least 5½ years, no advance repayment,
interest rate adjustable only once, after 5 years; or (2) last repayment after at least 7 years, average maturity at least 5½ years, no
advance repayment or adjustment of initial interest rate/. Otherwise,
financial credits are permitted only if the proceeds are used abroad,
either for direct investment (which is considered to include the purchase of ships and aircraft) or for repayment of earlier - licensed -
borrowings.

   k) Capital outflows via placing liquid assets with non-resident
      banks

     Resident non-banks may freely hold bank balances abroad,
whether in foreign or domestic currency, increasing by up to Fl. 10 million per year per foreign bank. The use of such balances for the
acquisition of unlisted guilder securities issued by non-residents is
prohibited. There is an obligation for holders of such accounts to
report regularly to the authorities.

Type of Regulation or Instrument / Type of Operation or Balance Sheet Position	Code	I. Exchange Control (1)	II. Minimum Reserve Require-ments	III. Interest Rate Control	IV. Pruden-tial Regula-tions	V. Tax Regula-tions	VI. Other Regula-tions or instru-ments
COMMERCIAL BANKS	1.						
Liability Operations/Positions	11.						
in foreign currencies	11.1						
with non-residents	11.11						
deposits from	11.111						
banks	11.111.1						
non-banks	11.111.2						
credits and loans from	11.112						
banks	11.112.1						
non-banks	11.112.2						
fixed-interest	11.113						
securities							
money market paper	11.113.1						
bonds	11.113.2	x					
with residents	11.12						
deposits from	11.121						
banks	11.121.1						
non-banks	11.121.2						
Central Bank or Government	11.121.3						
in domestic currency	11.2						
with non-residents	11.21						
current accounts of	11.211						
banks	11.211.1						
non-banks	11.211.2						
time deposits from	11.212						
banks	11.212.1						
non-banks	11.212.2						
credits and loans from	11.213						
banks	11.213.1						
non-banks	11.213.2						
fixed-interest securi-ties	11.214	x					
money market paper	11.214.1						
bonds	11.214.2						
Asset Operations/Positions	12.						
in foreign currencies	12.1						
with non-residents	12.11						
banks	12.111						
current accounts	12.111.1						
time deposits	12.111.2						
credits and loans	12.111.3						
non-banks	12.112						
credits and loans	12.112.1	x					
securities	12.113						
with residents	12.12						
deposits with banks	12.121						
credits and loans to non-banks	12.122						
securities	12.123						
deposits with Central bank	12.124						

(1) And similar regulations imposing quantitative controls on capital transactions with non-residents.

(Continued)

THE NETHERLANDS

(situation at the end of 1980)

Type of Operation or Balance Sheet Position / Type of Regulation or Instrument	Code	I. Exchange Control (1)	II. Minimum Reserve Requirements	III. Interest Rate Control	IV. Prudential Regulations	V. Tax Regulations	VI. Other Regulations or instruments
in domestic currency	12.2						
with non-residents	12.21						
deposits with banks	12.211						
credits and loans to	12.212						
banks	12.212.1						
non-banks	12.212.2	x					
securities	12.213	x					
Net Positions	13.						
in foreign currencies	13.1						x
vis-à-vis non-residents	13.2						
NON-BANKS	2.						
Liability Operations/Positions	21.						
credits and loans from	21.1						
non-resident banks	21.11	x					
in foreign currencies	21.111						
in domestic currency	21.112						
resident banks	21.12						
in foreign currencies	21.121						
Asset Operations/Positions	22.						
with non-resident banks	22.1	x					
in foreign currencies	22.11						
current accounts	22.111						
time deposits	22.112						
in domestic currency	22.12						
deposits	22.121						
with resident banks	22.2						
in foreign currencies	22.21						
current accounts	22.211						
time deposits	22.212						
FOREIGN EXCHANGE OPERATIONS/POSITIONS	3.						
Commercial Banks	31.						
spot foreign exchange dealings	31.1						
forward foreign exchange dealings	31.2						
swap transactions	31.3						x
net foreign exchange positions	31.4						
Non-Banks	32.						
spot foreign exchange dealings	32.1						
forward foreign exchange dealings	32.2	x					
swap transactions	32.3	x					

(1) And similar regulations imposing quantitative controls on capital transactions with non-residents.

IV. LISTING OF REGULATIONS BY CATEGORIES AND OPERATIONS
OR BALANCE SHEET POSITIONS

(situation at the end of 1980)

Code No. of classification schema	Operation/Position	Regulation
	I. EXCHANGE CONTROL	
I/11.113.2 I/11.214	Commercial banks issuing bonds, notes and money market paper abroad.	The issue of bonds and notes is subject to authorisation by the Netherlands Bank which is normally granted. The sale of short-term guilder money market paper (e.g. bankers' acceptances), and the assignment of guilder claims on residents to non-residents is prohibited.
I/12.112.1) I/12.212.2)	Commercial banks granting credits and loans in foreign currencies or domestic currency to non-resident non-banks (including internationally syndicated euro-credits).	Credits and loans up to 12 months may be freely granted as well as credits and loans of 12 months and over up to Fl. 10 million per year per foreign debtor. Additional amounts are permitted under general authorisation.
I/12.213	Commercial banks buying unlisted guilder securities (e.g. notes) issued by non-residents.	Freely permitted on condition that the securities in question are resold to non-residents.
I/21.11	Resident non-banks borrowing foreign currencies or domestic currency from foreign banks.	Subject to individual licence by the Netherlands Bank which is granted for commercial credits only if they are directly connected with specific commercial transactions with non-residents. Transfer of proceeds of financial credits is permitted only if they are from long term loans that meet specified conditions regarding minimum maturities and interest. Otherwise, financial credits are permitted only, if proceeds are used abroad. Fl. 500,000 a year are freely permitted.

Code No. of classification schema	Operation/Position	Regulation
I/22.1	Resident non-banks holding deposits in foreign currencies and domestic currency with foreign banks.	Freely permitted is an increase of up to Fl.10 million per year per foreign bank; otherwise, subject to individual licence which is normally granted. Account holders have to report regularly.
I/32.2) I/32.3)	Forward foreign-exchange operations of non-banks involving domestic currency (including swaps).	Forward guilder transactions against foreign currencies have to be passed through authorised banks.

VI. OTHER REGULATIONS OR INSTRUMENTS

(a) Understanding between the Netherlands Bank and commercial banks on foreign exchange positions

VI/13.1   Commercial banks' net foreign exchange positions.

The authorised banks are obliged to comply with requests from the Netherlands Bank - on the basis of extensive and frequent informa- tion supplied by them - to reduce or eliminate uncovered positions in any individual foreign currency (i.e. to balance their spot and for- ward positions in each currency vis-à-vis residents and non-residents taken together) if the Bank considers such open positions too large or protracted.

(b) Central bank swap facilities

VI/31.3   Commercial banks repatriating foreign currency assets on swap basis (inward switching).

With a view to achieving a temporary easing of the domestic money market situa- tion, the Netherlands Bank may provide at its discretion swap facilities for commercial banks' inward switching operations.

V. PRINCIPAL SOURCES OF LEGAL AND
REGULATORY PROVISIONS

Exchange Controls (and similar regulations imposing quantitative
limitations on capital operations with non-residents)

Exchange Control Decree of 1945, of 10th October, 1945

General Order of 1977 concerning Exchange Transactions, of
23rd March, 1977 (effective as from 1st September, 1977)

Note: Detailed rules of application are issued by the Netherlands
Bank in the form of Exchange Control Notices and General
Permissions.

Other Regulations or Instruments

a) Foreign-exchange cover requirements applying to
commercial banks

Exchange Control Decree 1945, of 10th October, 1945
(written understanding between the Netherlands Bank and
each individual bank)

b) Central bank swap facilities
Bank Act, of 23rd April, 1948.

SWEDEN

I. INTRODUCTION

(i)   Main characteristics of the regulatory system

The main restrictions on international banking transactions of
banks and non-banks in Sweden are the exchange control regulations.
Exchange controls are applied in order to support monetary policy and
for balance of payments reasons. Supervision of bank transactions in
foreign currencies, in order to ensure that the banks observe sound
banking practices and do not expose themselves unduly to exchange
risks, is performed by both the Sveriges Riksbank (the central bank
of Sweden) and the Bank Inspection Board. Minimum reserve requirements are used as instruments for monetary policy and are not designed
to affect international banking transactions in particular.

The legal basis for the Swedish exchange control system implies
that all transactions which have not been explicitly exempted require
authorisation by the Sveriges Riksbank. Two major exemptions can be
noted namely current payments and suppliers' credits. A great number
of general licences are also applied. In practice the exchange control
regulations are confined to capital movements, especially portfolio
investments. The regulations cover both inward and outward transactions
and concentrate on short-term transactions. Whereas the regulations
for short-term transactions have in the main been unchanged during the
years, those concerning long-term transactions have been changed more
freely. Credits financing Swedish foreign trade are in principle
allowed.

On the capital import side there has been a shift in emphasis
in exchange controls. Since 1974 Sweden has been experiencing
current account deficits. The restrictions on long-term borrowing
abroad have since then been eased considerably in order to facilitate
external financing of the deficits. Banks' liabilities resulting
from the refinancing abroad of domestic lending in foreign currencies
have also been exempted from reserve requirements since 1975.

75

Capital inflows other than long-term borrowing abroad and foreign direct investment in Sweden have remained more strictly controlled. Non-residents are in principle not allowed to buy domestic securities. Furthermore, there is practically no scope for inward switching operations by authorised banks(1) as their net foreign-currency assets always must be kept between two limits individually set for each bank.

Capital exports are closely controlled. Lending to non-residents, with the exception of commercial credits, is generally not permitted. Residents' purchases abroad of foreign securities are as a rule not allowed. Non-residents have only in a few special cases been allowed to issue securities on the domestic market. Resident non-banks' possibilities to hold liquid balances with foreign banks are limited as licences for such transactions are granted only restrictively. Authorised banks' outward switching operations are restricted as each bank's net foreign-currency assets must not exceed a certain limit. It should be noted that direct investments abroad are treated rather liberally although it is usually required that investments in other companies than sales subsidiaries be financed by foreign loans.

A number of regulations are aimed at warding off short-term potentially destabilizing inward and outward capital movements. Lending to non-residents is in principle prohibited with certain exceptions for commercial credits on normal payments terms. Non-residents may hold kronor-balances with resident banks, but they are partly discouraged from this since the balances as a rule must not be remunerated and must not be unusually large. Residents may deposit their foreign-currency receipts with resident banks, but the remuneration of such deposits requires an individual licence, which is granted only in special cases.

(ii)   Selected data on international banking operations

Sweden lacks significance as a centre of international banking activity. The low level of participation in international banking business in domestic and foreign currencies is due to exchange control regulations.

---

(1) Comprise all commercial banks, three of the largest savings banks and the Post Office.

Between end -1973 and end -1979 total foreign assets and liabilities of banks located in Sweden rose from US $ 1,93 billion to US $ 5,81 billion and from US $ 1,36 billion to US $ 8,71 billion, respectively.

At the end of 1973 the banks reported a small net asset position (US $ 0,57 billion) while at the end of 1978 there was a net liabilities position (US $ 2,90 billion). As for the domestic currency position a slight net liability (US $ 0,24 billion) in 1973 turned to a minor net asset position (US $ 0,13 billion) in 1979 Net assets in foreign currencies amounted to US 0,81 billion at the end of 1973, but at the end of 1978 the banks reported a net liabilities position in foreign currencies amounting to US $ 3,03 billion.

At the end of 1973, taking the Swedish banking system as a whole, foreign assets accounted for almost 9½ per cent of banks' balance sheet totals, while at the end of 1979 this ratio was about 11 per cent. The ratio of foreign liabilities to balance sheet totals rose from about 6 per cent to almost 14 per cent during the same period, reflecting increased borrowing abroad for domestic relending(1).

The Swedish krona is unimportant as a eurocurrency which is in line with policy intentions.

II. ANALYSIS OF REGULATIONS BY MAIN TYPES OF CAPITAL MOVEMENTS

(i) Commercial banks' foreign-currency operations
     a) External foreign-currency borrowing for relending abroad

Foreign-currency borrowing and lending operations with non-residents are normally subject to authorisation by the Riksbank. Licences have in some cases been granted for participation in internationally syndicated loans. In these cases the Riksbank has required that the participating Swedish banks refinance themselves abroad.

International money market transactions with non-residents for the purpose of interest arbitrage between two foreign currencies or one foreign currency and Swedish kronor are not permitted. However, authorised banks may take foreign-currency deposits from non-residents provided that the deposits received are redeposited with foreign banks in the same currency. The foreign-currency deposits received by authorised banks from non-residents may be remunerated.

---

(1) The ratios mentioned are derived from data published in the IMF International Financial Statistics on Commercial Banks

b) Capital inflows via inward switching

There is in principle no scope for capital inflows via authorised banks switching foreign-currency assets into domestic currency for their own account. First, authorised banks' net spot foreign-currency assets must be kept within a certain interval. Two limits are individually set for each bank - one minimum limit and one maximum limit between which the bank's net spot foreign-currency assets must be kept. Second, authorised banks are not allowed, without special licence, to create a net spot foreign-currency liability in any single currency by taking deposits or raising funds in order to switch the proceeds to kronor.

c) Capital inflows via the use of foreign-currency-funds raised abroad for granting foreign-currency loans to resident non-banks

Authorised banks may borrow foreign-currency funds abroad for relending to resident non-banks for the financing of Swedish foreign trade.

The same type of borrowing may take place for relending to Swedish companies which have been permitted to borrow abroad.

Loans to primarily small and medium-sized Swedish companies, not exceeding the equivalent of 10 million kronor in the individual case, for any purpose (with a few exceptions) in Sweden, may be granted without individual permission.

Loans granted to Swedish companies, other than loans financing Swedish foreign trade, normally must have an average maturity of at least 5 years. The authorised banks must refinance such loans abroad during the lifetime of the loans, but the refinancing may be made on a roll-over basis.

d) Capital outflows via outward switching

The scope for capital outflows via authorised banks switching domestic currency into foreign-currency assets for their own account is limited as each bank's net holdings of spot foreign-currency assets must not exceed a maximum limit (see section (i) b) above).

e) Capital outflows via financing external foreign-currency assets with foreign-currency deposits from resident non-banks

Residents are permitted to hold foreign-currency deposits with authorised banks. Such foreign-currency deposits (as well as foreign-currency deposits from non-residents) must be covered by deposits with foreign banks. Remuneration of foreign-currency deposits from residents is normally not allowed.

(ii) Commercial banks' domestic-currency operations with non-residents

f) Domestic-currency liabilities to non-residents

Authorised banks may accept deposits in domestic currency from non-residents provided that the deposits would not create balances which can be characterised as unusually large. The accounts must not be remunerated apart from certain exemptions applying to accounts of private individuals.

g) Placing domestic-currency funds with foreign banks

Authorised banks are not allowed to hold Swedish kronor balances with foreign banks. The Swedish banks are thus prevented from actively supplying Swedish kronor to the euromarket.

h) Domestic-currency credits and loans to non-residents

As a general rule authorised banks are not allowed to grant loans in domestic currency to non-residents.

It should be mentioned in this context, however, that according to a general licence authorised banks may permit normal overdrafts on External Kronor Accounts.

Furthermore, authorised banks are allowed to extend credits of not more than 6 months's maturity to foreign banks for the financing of Swedish exports and imports. In the case of Swedish exports the kronor amount must be transferred directly to the Swedish exporter.

The Riksbank also regularly allows authorised banks, upon individual application, to extend credits to foreign counterparts of Swedish exporters and importers or their banks for the financing of Swedish trade. In the case of Swedish exports the kronor amount must be transferred directly to the Swedish exporter. The Riksbank does not allow refinancing abroad in domestic currency.

(iii) <u>Non-bank borrowing and lending operations with non-resident banks</u>

j) <u>Capital inflows via borrowing from non-resident banks</u>

Residents' borrowing from non-resident banks requires prior authorisation from the Riksbank. Such authorisation is normally given for the financing of commercial transactions.

Resident non-banks may also receive permission to raise long-term loans abroad for any purpose (with a few exceptions) in Sweden.

Swedish shipyards are as a rule granted licences to borrow abroad to finance their shipbuilding in Sweden and to refinance their own credits to the buyers. Swedish shipping companies are normally granted licences to borrow abroad to finance purchases of ships in Sweden and abroad.

Local authorities and institutions for lending to such authorities may be granted licences for long-term borrowing abroad.

When a licence for direct investment abroad is granted the financing by borrowing abroad is permitted and in many cases prescribed by the Riksbank.

k) <u>Capital outflows via placing liquid assets with non-resident banks</u>

Resident non-banks' accounts with non-resident banks are subject to individual licenses.

Such licences are granted restrictively. However, according to a general licence insurance companies may hold accounts abroad.

III. SUMMARY VIEW OF REGULATIONS AND INSTRUMENTS AFFECTING INTERNATIONAL
BANKING OPERATIONS OF BANKS AND NON-BANKS IN

<u>SWEDEN</u>

(situation at the end of 1980)

Type of Operation or Balance Sheet Position / Type of Regulation or Instrument	Code	I. Exchange Control (1)	II. Minimum Reserve Require-ments	III. Interest Rate Control	IV. Pruden-tial Regula-tions	V. Tax Regula-tions	VI. Other Regula-tions or instru-ments
COMMERCIAL BANKS	1.						
Liability Operations/Positions	11.						
in foreign currencies	11.1						
with non-residents	11.11						
deposits from	11.111	x					
banks	11.111.1						
non-banks	11.111.2						
credits and loans from	11.112	x					
banks	11.112.1						
non-banks	11.112.2						
fixed-interest securities	11.113	x					
money market paper	11.113.1						
bonds	11.113.2						
with residents	11.12						
deposits from	11.121	x		x			
banks	11.121.1						
non-banks	11.121.2						
Central Bank or Government	11.121.3						
in domestic currency	11.2						
with non-residents	11.21						
current accounts of	11.211	x		x			
banks	11.211.1						
non-banks	11.211.2						
time deposits from	11.212	x		x			
banks	11.212.1						
non-banks	11.212.2						
credits and loans from	11.213	x					
banks	11.213.1						
non-banks	11.213.2						
fixed-interest securi-ties	11.214	x					
money market paper	11.214.1						
bonds	11.214.2						
Asset Operations/Positions	12.						
in foreign currencies	12.1						
with non-residents	12.11						
banks	12.111						
current accounts	12.111.1						
time deposits	12.111.2						
credits and loans	12.111.3	x					
non-banks	12.112						
credits and loans	12.112.1	x					
securities	12.113	x					
with residents	12.12						
deposits with banks	12.121						
credits and loans to non-banks	12.122	x					
securities	12.123	x					
deposits with Central bank	12.124						

(1) And similar regulations imposing quantitative controls on capital transactions
with non-residents.

III. SUMMARY VIEW OF REGULATIONS AND INSTRUMENTS AFFECTING INTERNATIONAL
(Continued)   BANKING OPERATIONS OF BANKS AND NON-BANKS IN

SWEDEN

(situation at the end of 1980)

Type of Operation or Balance Sheet Position / Type of Regulation or Instrument	Code	I. Exchange Control (1)	II. Minimum Reserve Requirements	III. Interest Rate Control	IV. Prudential Regulations	V. Tax Regulations	VI. Other Regulations or instruments
in domestic currency	12.2						
with non-residents	12.21						
deposits with banks	12.211	x					
credits and loans to	12.212						
banks	12.212.1	x					
non-banks	12.212.2	x					
securities	12.213	x					
Net Positions	13.						
in foreign currencies	13.1	x					
vis-à-vis non-residents	13.2						
NON-BANKS	2.						
Liability Operations/Positions	21.						
credits and loans from	21.1						
non-resident banks	21.11						
in foreign currencies	21.111	x					
in domestic currency	21.112	x					
resident banks	21.12						
in foreign currencies	21.121	x					
Asset Operations/Positions	22.						
with non-resident banks	22.1						
in foreign currencies	22.11	x					
current accounts	22.111						
time deposits	22.112						
in domestic currency	22.12	x					
deposits	22.121						
with resident banks	22.2						
in foreign currencies	22.21	x					
current accounts	22.211						
time deposits	22.212						
FOREIGN EXCHANGE OPERATIONS/POSITIONS	3.						
Commercial Banks	31.	x					x
spot foreign exchange dealings	31.1	x					
forward foreign exchange dealings	31.2	x					
swap transactions	31.3	x					
net foreign exchange positions	31.4	x					
Non-Banks	32.	x					
spot foreign exchange dealings	32.1						
forward foreign exchange dealings	32.2	x					
swap transactions	32.3						

(1) And similar regulations imposing quantitative controls on capital transactions with non-residents.

Code No. of classification schema	Operation/Position	Regulation

I. EXCHANGE CONTROL

I/11/112	Commercial banks raising credits and loans in foreign-currency from non-residents.	See I/12.122 Moreover, authorised banks may apply for a licence for the refinancing of commercial credits granted to non-residents.
I/11.113	Commercial banks issuing fixed-interest securities in foreign currency to non-residents.	Authorised banks' issues abroad of fixed-interest securities in foreign currency are subject to authorisation by the Riksbank. Authorisation is normally not granted for the issue of fixed-interest securities maturing within less than 5 years. As part of the raising of funds abroad for relending to residents, banks may however, obtain permission to issue commercial paper abroad.
I/11/111) I/11.121)	Commercial banks taking foreign-currency deposits from non-residents and residents.	Authorised banks may according to a general licence take foreign-currency deposits. There is an obligation for the authorised banks to cover such liabilities by depositing corresponding amounts and currencies with foreign banks. These deposits may have a maturity of up to 6 months. They may, however, have longer maturity to the extent that they cover deposits taken with corresponding maturity. These rules are supplemented by a provision that the banks should observe a reasonable maturity correspondence between foreign-currency deposits taken and given respectively. Deposits from non-residents employed for the purpose of financing the foreign-currency credits dealt with in item 12.122 are exempted from the above-mentioned cover obligation.

Code No. of classification schema	Operation/Position	Regulation
I/11.211) I/11.212)	Commercial banks taking deposits in domestic currency from non-residents.	Permitted under general licence. The deposits must not create unusually large balances.
I/11.213	Commercial banks raising credits and loans in domestic-currency from non-residents.	Generally prohibited.
I/11.214	Commercial banks issuing fixed-interest securities in domestic currency to non-residents.	Authorised banks' issues abroad of fixed-interest securities in domestic currency are generally prohibited.
I/12.111.3) I/12.112.1)	Commercial banks granting credits and loans in foreign-currency to non-resident banks or non-banks.	Generally not permitted. A loan to (or a deposit with) a foreign bank may, however, freely be made to the extent that it is financed by deposits in the same currency. The loan (deposit) may have a maturity of more than 6 months only if it is financed by a deposit of the same maturity. Authorised banks may also be licensed to grant credit to the foreign counterpart of a Swedish importer or exporter or to the foreign counterpart's bank. The underlying transaction must be in accordance with normal commercial practice.
I/12.113	Commercial banks' operations in securities in foreign currency issued by non-residents	The purchase abroad of foreign securities in foreign currency is subject to authorisation by the Riksbank. Authorisation is as a rule not granted. However, authorised banks have been granted individual licences to hold bonds denominated in foreign currency in order to enable them to participate in international bond issues and also to make purchases on the secondary market. The licences limit the holdings and prescribe refinancing abroad. In addition, authorised banks may include certain short-term securities in the net foreign-currency assets which they are allowed to hold (see I/13.1 and I/31.4).

Code No. of classification schema	Operation/Position	Regulation
I/12.113 (cont'd.)		Authorised banks may sell fixed-interest securities in foreign currency held by Swedish residents to abroad.
I/12.122	Commercial banks granting foreign-currency credits and loans to resident non-banks	Authorised banks may borrow foreign-currency funds abroad for relending to resident non-banks in the following cases:
		1. Credits not exceeding 6 months to Swedish exporters and importers to finance export credits and imports respectively. No. special permission is needed.
		2. Credits to primarily small and medium-sized enterprises for any purpose (with a few exceptions) in Sweden and for the financing of direct investments abroad. The individual credit must not exceed the equivalent of 10 million kronor and the average maturity of the loan must not be below 5 years. No special permission is needed.
		3. In cases where an enterprise has obtained a licence to borrow abroad, a bank may receive the permission to raise the funds abroad and relend them to the enterprise. The financing abroad must be upheld during the period of the relending but may consist of several consecutive shorter loans.
I/12.123	Commercial banks acquiring securities in foreign currency issued by residents.	The purchase abroad of Swedish securities in foreign-currency is subject to authorisation by the Riksbank, which is normally not granted.
I/12.211	Commercial banks holding domestic-currency deposits with foreign banks.	Prohibited.

Code No. of classification schema	Operation/Position	Regulation
I/12.212.1) I/12.212.2)	Commercial banks granting loans and credits in domestic-currency to non-residents.	As a general rule authorised banks are not allowed to grant loans in domestic currency to non-residents. However, credits financing Swedish foreign trade are in principle allowed, under certain conditions by means of general licences. Otherwise, approval is given on a case by case basis. The credits must be in accordance with normal commercial practice. Refinancing abroad in domestic currency is not allowed. According to a general licence, authorised banks may permit normal overdrafts on External Kronor Accounts.
I/12.213	Commercial banks acquiring securities in domestic currency issued by non-residents.	There exist very few securities in domestic currency issued by non-residents. The acquisition of such securities from non-residents would require authorisation from the Riksbank.
I/21.111	Resident non-banks raising loans and credits from non-resident banks in foreign currency	Residents' borrowing from non-resident banks requires prior authorisation from the Riksbank. Such authorisation is normally granted for the financing of commercial transactions. Swedish shipyards are as a rule granted licences to borrow abroad to finance their shipbuilding in Sweden and to refinance their own credits to the buyers. Swedish hipping companies are normally granted licences to borrow abroad to finance purchases of ships in Sweden and abroad. Resident non-banks may also receive permission to raise long-term loans abroad for any purpose (with a few exceptions) in Sweden. Local authorities and institutions for lending to such authorities may be granted licences for long-term borrowing abroad. Financing by borrowing abroad is permitted and in many cases prescribed by the Riksbank when a licence for a direct investment abroad is granted.

Code No. of classification schema	Operation/Position	Regulation
I/21.111 (cont'd.)		In the three last cases the maturity of the loans must not be less than 5 years on average.
I/21.112	Resident non-banks raising loans and credits from non-resident banks in domestic currency	Generally prohibited.
I/21.121	Resident non-banks raising loans and credits from resident banks in foreign currency .	See I/12.122.
I/22.11	Resident non-banks holding deposits in foreign currencies with non-resident banks.	Requires an individual licence. (Exempted from this rule are insurance companies.) Licences are granted restrictively.
I/22.12	Resident non-banks holding deposits in domestic currency with non-resident banks.	Generally prohibited.
I/22.21	Resident non-banks holding foreign-currency deposits with resident banks.	When a resident receives a free or licensed payment in a foreign currency, he may deposit it with an authorised bank according to a general licence. There is no time limit for such deposits, but as a rule they must not be remunerated.
I/31	Commercial banks' foreign exchange dealings.	Only authorised banks are allowed to deal in foreign exchange. Authorisation is granted by the Sveriges Riksbank.
I/31.1	Commercial banks' spot foreign exchange dealings.	Authorised banks may purchase foreign exchange from and sell foreign exchange to resident non-banks, but only for authorised purposes.
		Spot foreign exchange dealings with foreign banks in foreign currency against kronor must not without permission be concluded for less than two days.

Code No. of classifica- tion schema	Operation/Position	Regulation
I/31.2	Commercial banks' forward foreign exchange dealings.	Authorised banks may conclude forward exchange transactions with each other. Forward exchange dealings with resident non-banks are subject to certain restrictions. See I/32.2
		Authorised banks may conclude forward contracts up to 12 months with foreign banks. Should, however, the contract be concluded against kronor in a currency other than the domestic currency of the foreign bank, a prerequisite is that the contract is intended to cover a forward exchange transaction between the authorised bank and a resident. Otherwise an individual licence is required.
		The maturities of forward contracts concluded with foreign banks may exceed 12 months if the contracts cover authorised forward transactions between the authorised bank and a resident.
		Authorised banks are not allowed to conclude forward exchange dealings with non-resident non-banks.
I/31.3	Commercial banks' swap transactions.	No special rules apply to swap transactions. See rules for authorised banks' spot and forward foreign exchange dealings (I/31.1 and 1/31.2).
I/13.1) I/31.4)	Commercial banks' net position in foreign currencies.	An authorised bank's spot net position in all foreign currencies taken together are subject to limitations. Two limits - a maximum limit and a minimum limit - are individually set for each bank. The banks are obliged to keep their net holdings of foreign currency assets between those limits and the net position in any single currency must be positive. When calculating the net holdings, claims on residents and non-resident non-banks as well as liabilities abroad intended for refinancing of lending to non-banks are excluded.
I/32	Foreign exchange transactions of resident non-banks.	There is a general obligation for resident non-banks to execute their foreign exchange transactions through authorised banks. Direct transactions with non-residents are as a rule not permitted.

Code No. of classification schema	Operation/Position	Regulation
I/32 (cont'd.)		Resident non-banks may buy foreign exchange from and sell foreign exchange to authorised banks for current or otherwise authorised payments.
I/32.2	Forward foreign exchange transactions of resident non-banks.	Resident non-banks may conclude forward exchange transactions with authorised banks in order to cover authorised payments. The forward contracts may be concluded

a) without time limits in respect of forward sales and of payments for imports, freights and charter services

b) for periods up to 12 months in respect of repayment of and interest on loans raised abroad for the refinancing of export credits grantedin kronor

c) for periods up to 6 months in respect of all other payments.

Resident non-banks' forward contracts with authorised banks may only be concluded against kronor. Authorised banks may, however, conclude forward exchange transactions direct between two foreign countries if conditions are at hand to sell forward a foreign currency to a resident non bank and to buy forward another foreign currency from the same resident and if the payments behind follow closely with regard to maturity. Further resident non banks who have raised a loan in foreign currency may under certain conditions buy forward the currency in which the loan is expressed against another foreign currency.

III. INTEREST RATE CONTROL(1)

III/11.121	Interest payments on commercial banks' deposits in foreign currency received from residents.	Remuneration of residents' foreign-currency accounts with authorised banks requires an individual licence which can be obtained only in special cases.
III/11.211) III/11.212)	Interest payments on commercial banks' domestic currency liabilities to non-residents.	Remuneration of non-residents' accounts in domestic currency with authorised banks is prohibited with a few exceptions applying mainly to accounts of individuals.

---

(1) The regulations mentioned under section III, Interest Rate Control, are issued for the purpose of foreign exchange control and thus properly assignable to section I.

VI. OTHER REGULATIONS OR INSTRUMENTS

VI/31	Commercial banks' foreign exchange dealings.	The Swedish Bank Inspection Board has issued the recommendation that at least 5% of the authorised bank's total spot foreign exchange turnover should be directly related to the bank's foreign exchange dealings with its customers.

V. PRINCIPAL SOURCES OF LEGAL AND REGULATORY PROVISIONS

Exchange Controls

Exchange Control Act of 22nd June, 1939 (Swedish Code of Statutes 1939:350)

Exchange Control Ordinance of 5th June, 1959 (Swedish Code of Statutes 1959:264)

Rules for the Application of the Exchange Control Ordinance. (Consecutively issued by the Sveriges Riksbank.)

SWITZERLAND

I. INTRODUCTION

i) Main purposes of the regulatory system

Traditionally, Switzerland has been a net exporter of private long-term capital and has, at the same time, functioned as an important international financial centre with close links to financial markets in other countries. But, given the small size of the domestic economy, net outflows of domestic capital, partly as a result of policy, have remained small in relation to the large amounts of funds which the Swiss financial centre has channelled from non-resident investors to non-resident borrowers. As interest rates have generally been low in comparison with other countries, in line with policy intentions, the authorities have, under normal conditions, been confronted with the problem of protecting the country's limited domestic financial resources against unduly large recourse by foreign borrowers and undesirably strong upward pressure on domestic interest rates which would result. This underlying situation explains why Switzerland has traditionally controlled certain relatively important channels for capital exports.

From the early sixties well into the late seventies, however, the Swiss authorities have repeatedly been faced with the opposite problem of protecting the small domestic economy and the exchange rate against destabilising effect of large speculative capital inflows, a task which was all the more difficult to accomplish as such flows quite frequently reached dimensions which were very large in relation to domestic monetary aggregates and bank liquidity. In coping with these relatively new problems the authorities made increasing use of intervention techniques restricting capital inflows which previously had not been applied, partly because Switzerland has traditionally adhered to the principle of freedom of capital movements and partly because the authorities, for constitutional reasons, had not been well equipped with adequate policy instruments.

With a view to discouraging massive capital inflows and, at the same time, counteracting upward pressures on the exchange rate, a whole range of new instruments was put into operation, among which:

- prohibition of remunerating non-resident Swiss-franc
  deposits and charging a "negative" interest rate on
  such accounts;

- quantitative limits on forward commitments in Swiss
  francs vis-à-vis non-residents serving the purpose
  of preventing the interest rate measure from being
  circumvented by the technique of non-resident swap
  deposits;

- prohibition of non-resident fiduciary accounts
  denominated in Swiss francs;

- restrictive control on non-bank borrowing abroad.

Some other forms of capital imports, notably the acquisition
by non-residents of Swiss domestic securities, and cash bonds
(Kassenobligationen) which are issued by banks, were left free
during most of this period of speculative capital inflows (1);
but a 35 per cent withholding tax on interest income from these
instruments provides a relatively strong disincentive under normal
conditions.

This restrictive regulatory framework was superimposed on the
existing set of traditional controls aimed at regulating total
capital exports in accordance with the country's capacity for net
exports of domestic financial resources. These controls apply to
specific types of outward capital operations: bank credits to
non-residents, foreign bond issues, foreign issue of medium-term
notes (private placements) which are subject to individual license.

These capital export controls have been used for regulating
the re-export of inflowing capital and achieving a corresponding
reduction in official reserves and central bank money supply. An
important provision in this respect was the requirement for non-
resident borrowers, now abolished, to convert the Swiss franc
borrowing proceeds into foreign exchange to be obtained from the
central bank. This latter measure, at the same time, served the
more general aim of the authorities to prevent the Swiss franc from
being too widely used internationally.

_____

(1) Only from June 1972 to February 1974 and from February 1978
    to January 1979 a ban on such purchases was enforced by the
    Swiss authorities.

Towards the end of 1978, in view of the adverse consequences of the continuing appreciation of the Swiss franc on the Swiss economy, the Swiss authorities decided upon an important change of policy and publicly declared to aim henceforth at particular quantitative exchange rate relationships. To this end, they expressed their willingness to create as much money as needed to maintain those stated exchange rates. At the beginning, this change in policy yet necessitated large-scale interventions on the foreign exchange market, but it subsequently contributed to the return of relative quiet on the markets and allowed a gradual easing and abolition of the various restrictive measures. As of end-December 1980 only the regulations concerning capital exports (based on Article 8 of the Federal Act on Banks and Savings Banks) were enforced.

Internationally, the Swiss franc has become the third most important euro-currency after the US dollar and the Deutsche mark, a development which the authorities in Switzerland have been unable to avoid. As exports of short-term funds by banks and non-banks in Swiss francs (as well as in foreign currencies) have remained free, Switzerland has been a relatively important source for supplying the euro-Swiss franc market.

In the absence of a developed domestic money market, the Swiss National Bank influences domestic liquidity mainly by buying and selling foreign assets. One important instrument in this respect is foreign currency swaps with commercial banks. 'Inward' swaps provide liquidity for a shorter or a longer period, while 'outward' swaps are used to reduce liquidity in the banking system. 'Outward' swaps are preferred over other sterilisation measures such as minimum-reserve requirements because they can be applied in a more flexible way.

With regard to foreign currencies, banks are free to accept deposits from residents and non-residents or to borrow funds from other, euro-market centres for relending abroad (within the limits of the capital export regulations) but there are certain obstacles which prevent them from participating flexibly and competitively in all kinds of euro-market operations, notably medium-term operations, which may explain why Switzerland's role as euro-market centre (not counting the banks' fiduciary business in euro-currencies) has remained relatively modest in the course of the seventies in contrast to developments in some other smaller countries with euro-market centres. The 35 per cent withholding tax provision is probably the most important disincentive to be mentioned in this context. Only short-term (i.e. up to one year) interbank transactions are exempted from this provision.

ii)   Selected data on international banking operations

Among the European countries reporting to the Bank for International Settlements, Switzerland, after the United Kingdom, France, Germany and Luxembourg but well in front of the Netherlands and Belgium, ranks fifth as a centre for international banking business (1). Though foreign-currency business is considerably more important than international banking operations in domestic currency, Switzerland is the second most important lender of domestic-currency funds in Europe (2). Switzerland's overall position as a net exporter of banking funds, taking domestic and foreign currencies together, has become even more important than that of France.

Between end-1973 and end-1979, total external assets and liabilities rose from US$ 17 billion to US$ 59.1 billion and from US$ 15.8 billion to US$ 38.2 billion, respectively. Most of the expansion took place in the foreign-currency sector; in fact, non-resident deposits in domestic currency actually increased only marginally as a result of the measures taken against inflows of foreign funds into Swiss franc deposits. Switzerland's share in international banking business has decreased marginally to some 7.7 per cent of total international bank lending at the end of 1979, the share in foreign deposit business dropping from 7.0 per cent to 5.0 per cent in the six-year period 1974-1979 (3). As a

---

(1) At the end of 1979, non-resident fiduciary accounts in foreign currencies amounted to the order of magnitude of some US$41 billion. Since investments in fiduciary assets do not reflect the banks' own lending decisions, fiduciary business is, for the purposes of this note, not considered as international banking business.

(2) After Germany in terms of gross assets and after France in terms of net assets.

(3) The market shares are measured as a percentage of total external assets and liabilities, respectively, of the banks of the European countries (counting Belgium and Luxembourg separately) reporting to the Bank for International Settlements.

euro-market centre Switzerland has about maintained its position
with its share in total foreign-currency deposits remaining stable
at a level of just below 5 per cent over recent years (1).

Between end-1973 and end-1979, reflecting a strong current
account balance, Switzerland recorded a sharp improvement in the
banks' net external asset position from just over US$ 1 billion to
close to US$ 21 billion (end-1979); the larger part of the increase
took place in the domestic-currency sector.

At the end of 1978, taking the Swiss banking system as a
whole, foreign business accounted for about 36.3 per cent on the
lending side i.e. somewhat more   in percentage terms than at the
end of 1973, and for about 26.8 per cent on the liabilities side
i.e. three percentage points less than six years earlier.

The Swiss franc is the third most important euro-currency
after the Deutsche Mark with a market share (1) in total euro-currency
business of about 6.0 per cent (end-1979); six years earlier the
share was considerably higher - 8.9 per cent. Similar to the situation in the Deutsche Mark sector, the offshore market for Swiss-franc
denominated assets and liabilities is considerably larger than the
amounts of foreign assets and liabilities of the Swiss banking system
in domestic currency (2). The main centres for euro-Swiss franc
business are located in London and Paris.

---

(1) The market share is measured as a percentage of total
    external foreign-currency liabilities of banks of the
    European countries (counting Belgium and Luxembourg
    separately) reporting to the Bank for International Settlements.

(2) At the end of 1979, Swiss franc assets and liabilities of
    banks outside Switzerland amounted to US$38.7 billion and
    US$40.7 billion respectively; and Swiss banks' external
    assets and liabilities in Swiss francs stood at US$27.2 billion
    and US$7.4 billion, respectively. Part of the Swiss franc
    assets of banks outside Switzerland are held with banks in
    Switzerland and thus fall outside the euro-market area.

II. ANALYSIS OF REGULATIONS BY MAIN TYPES OF CAPITAL MOVEMENTS

(situation at the end of 1980)

i)   Commercial banks' foreign-currency operations

a) External foreign-currency borrowing for relending abroad

Commercial banks' external foreign-currency borrowing for relending abroad is adversely affected by a 35 per cent withholding tax,
which, in principle, non-residents - as well as residents - have to pay
on interest received from holdings of bank deposits, whether in domestic
or foreign currency, or of other financing instruments issued by residents such as marketable bonds and cash bonds (Kassenobligationen).
Residents may reclaim the withholding tax as a tax credit; non-residents may only do so in cases where double taxation agreements exist.
Exempted from the withholding tax requirement are only domestic and
foreign banks in respect of interest payments received on deposits
(in domestic or foreign currency) with effective maturities of up
to one year.   Thus, foreign-currency bank lending to non-residents
is free of obstacles only to the extent that it is re-financed in the
international market for short-term interbank funds.

Minimum-reserve requirements on external liabilities have not
been used since end-February 1977; if applied the Swiss National Bank
may decide that for minimum-reserve purposes foreign-currency claims
on non-residents are deductible from foreign-currency liabilities to
non-residents.

Bank credits and loans to non-resident banks or non-banks
exceeding the equivalent of Sw.fr. 10 million each and with a maturity of 12 months and more require prior permission of the Swiss
National Bank.

On balance, banks in Switzerland are not very actively engaged
in the international syndication of medium-term euro-credits, but they
participate in such operations indirectly via their foreign branches,
subsidiaries and joint ventures.

b) Capital inflows via inward switching

The use by banks of foreign-currency funds originating from
non-resident depositors or lenders for switching into Swiss francs
has been subject to quantitative limitations since November 1974. At
the end of 1979, forward foreign-currency claims on non-residents

arising from forward sales of Swiss francs to non-residents for maturities of ten days and less were limited to 20 per cent of the amounts outstanding on 31st October, 1974 and those with maturities of over ten days to 50 per cent of the said amounts. These restrictions were liberalized in February 1980 and abolished in March.

Though the measure was essentially designed to prevent circumvention of the prohibition of interest payment and of the charging of a commission on non-resident Swiss franc deposits (see section ii) f) below), it limits at the same time the banks' scope for switching foreign-currency funds on a swap basis into Swiss franc assets.

It should be noted that the ceilings mentioned above applied only to the banks' Swiss franc forward liabilities to non-residents and have no effect on swaps concluded with the central bank. The Swiss National Bank, in fact, frequently provides special cover facilities for "inward" swaps which are flexibly used as an instrument of domestic money market policy and which may ensure the re-export of foreign-currency funds that banks may wish to repatriate for meeting temporary domestic liquidity needs.

c) Capital inflows via the use of foreign-currency funds raised abroad for granting foreign-currency loans to resident non-banks

Until end-February 1977, this type of capital inflow was impaired by minimum-reserve requirements on foreign-currency liabilities which tended to increase the cost of intermediation of the banks and hence interest rates on the domestic banks' foreign-currency loans to resident borrowers as compared with those charged by foreign banks. Given the relatively low effective reserve ratios which were in force at that time, such cost effects had not been very important.

d) Capital outflows via outward switching

There are no obstacles to capital outflows via banks switching Swiss francs into foreign-currency assets. The banks in Switzerland, taken as a whole, are in fact holders of a considerable net external assets positions in foreign currencies. Since a relatively recent period, the Swiss National Bank provides facilities for "outward" swaps which, together with "inward" swap facilities, are used for influencing monetary aggregates and domestic interest rates. "Outward" swaps, in particular, are aimed at mopping up excess liquidity created by official foreign-exchange market intervention operations, notably in situations where other "sterilisation" measures such as the use of minimum-reserve requirements are considered as not, or not yet, appropriate.

e) Capital outflows via financing external foreign-currency assets with foreign-currency deposits from resident non-banks

At the end of 1980, no obstacles existed to this type of capital outflow. Since November 1974, resident deposits (whether in domestic or foreign currency) have no longer been subject to minimum-reserve requirements. Resident non-banks hold, in fact, substantial amounts of net foreign-currency claims on banks in Switzerland.

ii) Commercial banks' domestic-currency operations with non-residents

f) Domestic-currency liabilities to non-residents

Banks' Swiss franc liabilities to non-residents up until the end of 1979 have been subject to considerable restrictions which were designed to impair the flow of foreign funds into the country and to discourage the demand for Swiss francs in foreign exchange markets.

Since 22nd January, 1975, the remuneration of Swiss franc deposits of non-resident banks and non-banks has been prohibited. Exempt from these interest rate regulations are savings and similar accounts of private individuals; such accounts outstanding at end-October 1974, plus an increase of Sw.fr. 100.000, or new accounts up to Sw.fr. 100.000 may be remunerated.

In February 1980, the ban on interest payments was removed for foreign savings deposits and time deposits of foreign central banks with a minimum maturity of six months; in March of this year this interest ban was abolished for all foreign time deposits with a minimum maturity of three months. In August 1980 the ban on interest payments was completely lifted.

Between end-1974 and end-1979, moreover, Swiss franc deposits of non-resident banks and non-banks, have been subject to special commission charges; these were abolished in December 1979.

Until February 1977, non-resident Swiss franc deposits with banks in Switzerland were subject to minimum-reserve requirements in the form of non-interest bearing special deposits to be held with the Swiss National Bank. Reserve ratios applied to both outstanding amounts and on the growth of eligible liabilities after end-July 1971 and end-October 1974, respectively. For the time being no use is made of reserve requirements, in part because other measures suitable for mopping up excess liquidity, including the use of central bank facilities for "outward" swaps are considered as being more flexible.

g) Placing domestic-currency funds with foreign banks

There are no obstacles to this type of capital outflow. Placements with maturities of one year and over and each amounting to Sw. Frs. 10 million and over require authorisation by the Swiss National Bank, which is normally granted.

h) Domestic-currency credits and loans to non-resident non-banks

Bank credits and loans with maturities of one year and over and each amounting to Sw. Frs. 10 million require prior authorisation by the Swiss National Bank, which is normally granted.

Memorandum Item:

Commercial banks' transactions with non-residents in fixed-interest securities denominated in domestic currency

The purchase by banks in Switzerland of non-resident new issues of bonds and notes denominated in Swiss francs is affected insofar as the following operations are subject to prior authorisation by the Swiss National Bank:

- new foreign Swiss franc bond issues in Switzerland each amounting to Sw. Frs. 10 million and more;
- new foreign issues of Swiss franc medium-term notes (private placements) in Switzerland each amounting to Sw. Frs. 3 million or more.

Authorisation is generally granted. New issues of foreign Swiss franc bonds and medium-term notes may be subject to ceilings fixed for specific periods; they presently are not.

Banks are free to deal with non-residents on secondary markets in domestic-currency denominated bonds. The latest instruction pamphlet of September 1, 1980, makes allowance for a limited secondary market for notes. Moreover, foreign banks and central banks have now the possibility of buying these securities under certain conditions. The aim of the Swiss National Bank is to have Swiss franc transactions channelled through Swiss banks. The information which should thus be obtained will facilitate the shaping of monetary policy by the Central Bank. The physical export of such notes is still prohibited.

iii) Non-bank borrowing and lending operations with non-residents banks

j) Capital inflows via borrowing from non-resident banks

Non-bank borrowing abroad, whether in domestic or foreign currency, which required prior authorisation by the Swiss National Bank until the end of May 1979, is no longer restricted.

k) Capital outflows via placing liquid assets with non-resident banks

Resident non-banks are entirely free to open accounts with foreign banks and to place liquid funds, whether in domestic or foreign currency, on foreign national money markets and the euro-market, including the euro-Swiss franc market. The application of a 35 per cent withholding tax on interest earned on domestic bank accounts provides an incentive for resident non-banks to hold liquid funds abroad, directly or via fiduciary accounts held with domestic banks.

III. SUMMARY VIEW OF REGULATIONS AND INSTRUMENTS AFFECTING INTERNATIONAL
BANKING OPERATIONS OF BANKS AND NON-BANKS IN

SWITZERLAND

(situation at the end of 1980)

Type of Operation or Balance Sheet Position / Type of Regulation or Instrument	Code	I. Exchange Control (1)	II. Minimum Reserve Requirements	III. Interest Rate Control	IV. Prudential Regulations	V. Tax Regulations	VI. Other Regulations or instruments
COMMERCIAL BANKS	1.						
Liability Operations/Positions	11.					x	
in foreign currencies	11.1						
with non-residents	11.11						
deposits from	11.111						
banks	11.111.1						
non-banks	11.111.2						
credits and loans from	11.112						
banks	11.112.1						
non-banks	11.112.2						
fixed-interest	11.113						
securities							
money market paper	11.113.1						
bonds	11.113.2						
with residents	11.12						
deposits from	11.121						
banks	11.121.1						
non-banks	11.121.2						
Central Bank or Government	11.121.3						
in domestic currency	11.2						
with non-residents	11.21						
current accounts of	11.211						
banks	11.211.1						
non-banks	11.211.2						
time deposits from	11.212						
banks	11.212.1						
non-banks	11.212.2						
credits and loans from	11.213						
banks	11.213.1						
non-banks	11.213.2						
fixed-interest securities	11.214						
money market paper	11.214.1						
bonds	11.214.2						
Asset Operations/Positions	12.						
in foreign currencies	12.1						
with non-residents	12.11						
banks	12.111	x					
current accounts	12.111.1						
time deposits	12.111.2						
credits and loans	12.111.3						
non-banks	12.112	x					
credits and loans	12.112.1						
securities	12.113	x					
with residents	12.12						
deposits with banks	12.121						
credits and loans to non-banks	12.122						
securities	12.123						
deposits with Central bank	12.124						

(1) And similar regulations imposing quantitative controls on capital transactions with non-residents.

(Continued)

(situation at the end of 1980)

Type of Operation or Balance Sheet Position / Type of Regulation or Instrument	Code	I. Exchange Control (1)	II. Minimum Reserve Requirements	III. Interest Rate Control	IV. Prudential Regulations	V. Tax Regulations	VI. Other Regulations or instruments
in domestic currency	12.2						
with non-residents	12.21						
deposits with banks	12.211	x					
credits and loans to	12.212	x					
banks	12.212.1						
non-banks	12.212.2						
securities	12.213	x					
Net Positions	13.						
in foreign currencies	13.1						
vis-à-vis non-residents	13.2						
NON-BANKS	2.						
Liability Operations/ Positions	21.						
credits and loans from	21.1						
non-resident banks	21.11						
in foreign currencies	21.111						
in domestic currency	21.112						
resident banks	21.12						
in foreign currencies	21.121						
Asset Operations/Positions	22.						
with non-resident banks	22.1						
in foreign currencies	22.11						
current accounts	22.111						
time deposits	22.112						
in domestic currency	22.12						
deposits	22.121						
with resident banks	22.2						
in foreign currencies	22.21						
current accounts	22.211						
time deposits	22.212						
FOREIGN EXCHANGE OPERATIONS/ POSITIONS	3.						
Commercial Banks	31.						
spot foreign exchange dealings	31.1						
forward foreign exchange dealings	31.2						
swap transactions	31.3						x
net foreign exchange positions	31.4						
Non-Banks	32.						
spot foreign exchange dealings	32.1						
forward foreign exchange dealings	32.2						
swap transactions	32.3						

(1) And similar regulations imposing quantitative controls on capital transactions with non-residents.

IV. LISTING OF REGULATIONS BY CATEGORIES AND BY OPERATIONS ON BALANCE SHEET POSITIONS

(situation at the end of 1980)

CODE No. OF CLASSIFICATION SCHEMA	OPERATION/POSITION	REGULATION
	I. EXCHANGE CONTROL	
I/12.111) I/12.211)	Commercial banks holding domestic and foreign currency deposits with foreign banks.	Time deposits with maturities of twelve months and over and exceeding Sw.Frs. 10 million or equivalent in foreign currency per individual operation require the permission of the Swiss National Bank.
I/12.112) I/12.212)	Commercial banks granting credits and loans in domestic and foreign currency to non-resident banks or non-banks.	Bank credits and loans exceeding Sw.Frs. 10 million or equivalent in foreign currency each and with a maturity of twelve months and more require the permission of the Swiss National Bank.
I/12.113) I/12.213)	Commercial banks buying newly issued foreign securities denominated in domestic and foreign currency.	The following operations are subject to prior authorisation by the Swiss National Bank: - foreign bond issues in domestic or foreign currency each amounting to Sw.Frs. 10 million or equivalent in foreign currency or more; - foreign issues of me medium-term notes (private placements) in domestic and foreign currency each amounting to Sw.Fras. 3 million or equivalent in foreign currency, or more.

V. TAX REGULATION

V/11

Interest payments on com-
mercial banks' liabilities
to non-residents and
residents in foreign
currencies and domestic
currency.

Subject to a 35 per cent
withholding tax which residents may reclaim as a tax
credit; non-residents may
do so only in cases where
double-taxation agreements
exist. Exempt from with-
holding tax requirements
are interest payments on
deposits from domestic
and foreign banks in do-
mestic and foreign cur-
rency with effective
maturities of up to one
year.

VI. OTHER REGULATIONS OR INSTRUMENTS

a) Central bank swap facilities

VI/31.3

Commercial banks' "inward"
and "outward" swap
transactions.

The Swiss National Bank
has used "inward" swaps
with commercial banks
for quite some time, and
"outward" swaps since a
more recent period, as
a monetary-policy
instrument serving the
regulation of monetary
aggregates and domestic
interest rates. "Inward"
swaps are intended to
ensure the re-export of
foreign currency funds
that banks may repatriate
for meeting temporary
domestic liquidity needs.
"Outward" swaps are used
for mopping up excess
liquidity created by
official foreign-exchange
market intervention
operations, notably in
situations where other
"sterilisation" measures
such as the use of
minimum-reserve require-
ments are considered as
not, or not yet,
appropriate.

V. PRINCIPAL SOURCES OF LEGAL AND REGULATORY PROVISIONS

Exchange Controls (and similar regulations imposing quantitative limitations on capital operations with non-residents)

1. Federal Act on Banks and Savings Banks of
   8th November, 1934/11th March, 1971 (Article 8)

2. Federal Act on the Swiss National Bank of
   23rd December, 1953/11th March, 1976/15th
   December, 1978

   Note: Detailed rules of application of capital export
   controls are issued by the Swiss National Bank
   in the form of instruction pamphlets.

Minimum Reserve Requirements

Federal Ordinance on Minimum reserve requirements of
banks of July 11, 1979

Tax Regulation

Federal Anticipatory Tax

Federal Act on the anticipatory tax of
13th October, 1965.   Ordinance to the
Federal Act on the anticipatory tax of
19th December, 1966.

THE UNITED KINGDOM

I. INTRODUCTION

i) Main purposes of regulatory system

The United Kingdom has experienced a number of phases of, at times considerable, pressure on its external payments position and on its exchange rate in connection with current account deficits, which were particularly large in the period 1973 to 1976, and capital outflows. Situations where excessive capital inflows tended to create problems for domestic monetary control have also occurred but less frequently.

Accordingly, from 1939 until October 1979 restrictions or special impediments were imposed on exports of resident capital; the regulations were aimed at limiting the scope for speculative outflows from sterling and conserving the foreign currency reserves. The nature and severity of the regulations fluctuated considerably over the years in line with the country's changing external financial position.

In more recent years it has been possible to introduce a process of progressive liberalisation of controls. This culminated in the removal on 23rd October, 1979 of all the remaining restrictions imposed under the Exchange Control Act 1947. Banks and non-banks are now free to remit funds abroad for any purpose and to buy, sell, borrow and retain foreign currency without restriction by the authorities who take a favourable view of London's development as a major euro-market centre. However, with the abolition of controls over banks' dealing positions in foreign currency against sterling, it has become necessary for prudential reasons to institute alternative arrangements for monitoring the foreign currency exposure of banks.

Although capital imports are free of restrictions, any resultant increase in a bank's 'eligible liabilities' is subject to minimum reserve and special deposit requirements. Banks which appear on the Bank of England's statistical list are required to hold specified reserve assets in a ratio previously of 12.5 per cent, but reduced from 5 January 1981 to 10 per cent, on total

'eligible liabilities'(1). The latter are, broadly, sterling
deposit liabilities (excluding those with an original maturity
of over two years), plus any sterling resources obtained by
switching from foreign currencies, sterling interbank transactions
and sterling CDS (held and issued) are also taken into account,
but on a net basis, and irrespective of term. Special deposits (on
which interest is paid) may be called by the Bank of England from
all banks subject to the reserve asset ratio requirement, although
there have been no special deposits outstanding since mid-January,
1980.

ii) Selected data on international banking operations

The United Kingdom is the biggest international banking
centre within the OECD area, mainly reflecting its important role
as a euro-market centre. International bank lending in sterling
remains small, although following the abolition of exchange control in October 1979, there has been significant growth. Sterling
deposits, however, have continued to play a certain role as international reserve balances. In the past, the United Kingdom has
made substantial use of its banking system's facilities for financing balance-of-payments deficits and as a result the U.K.
banking system still has large net external liabilities in foreign
currencies.

In the period from end-1973 to end-1979, the banks' total
external assets and liabilities - essentially in foreign currencies - rose from US$ 85.7 billion to US$ 285.5 billion and
from US$ 96.8 billion to US$ 301.2 billion, respectively; however, in the face of competition from other European countries and
the offshore centres, the United Kingdom's market share fell from
about 43.5% to 38.9% on the liabilities side, and on the assets
side declined from 40.9% at end-1973 to 36.8% at end-1979(2).

---

(1) The London Clearing Banks are currently required to hold
    non-interest-bearing balances at the Bank of England
    equivalent to a minimum of 1½ per cent of their eligible
    liabilities.

(2) The market shares are measured as a percentage of total
    external assets and liabilities of banks of the European
    countries (counting Belgium and Luxembourg separately)
    reporting to the Bank for International Settlements.

In euro-currency deposit business the United Kingdom market share also declined from 47.8% to 42.3%(1).

In comparison with domestic business, international operations of the United Kingdom banking system have expanded considerably in recent years with foreign assets and liabilities as a ratio of the balance sheet total rising from 50.2% to 64.3% on the asset side and from 54.5% to 67.9% on the liabilities side between end-1973 and end-1978(2).

Deposits of euro-sterling increased in importance between 1976 and 1979, rising from US$ 4.0 billion to US$ 15.3 billion. During the same period non-resident sterling deposits with United Kingdom banks rose from US$ 7.1 billion to US$ 19.2 billion. At end-1979 total euro-sterling deposits accounted for 2.3% of total euro-currency deposits, as compared with 2.4% at end 1973(3). This compares with a ratio of 17.5% for euro-deutschemarks and 6.1% for euro-Swiss francs. The main centres for euro-sterling business are located in France, the Netherlands and Belgium-Luxembourg.

II. ANALYSIS OF REGULATIONS BY MAIN TYPES OF CAPITAL MOVEMENTS

(situation at the end of 1980)

(i) Commercial banks' foreign-currency operations

(a) External foreign-currency borrowing for relending abroad

Banks are entirely free to take foreign-currency deposits or to raise foreign-currency credits from non-resident banks and non-banks for the purpose of re-employing these funds abroad in foreign-currency banking transactions: foreign-currency deposits

---

(1) The market share is measured as a percentage of total external foreign currency liabilities of banks of the European countries (counting Belgium and Luxembourg separately) reporting to the Bank for International Settlements.

(2) The ratios mentioned are derived from data published in IMF International Financial Statistics on Deposit Money Banks which exclude domestic inter-bank deposits both in foreign and domestic currency.

(3) The market share is measured as a percentage of total external foreign currency liabilities of banks of the European countries (counting Belgium and Luxembourg separately) reporting to the Bank for International Settlements.

with foreign banks, money market or security market investments,
or loans including internationally syndicated euro-loans. Banks
are also free to raise, or employ, such foreign-currency funds in
the domestic foreign-currency interbank market, which is an essential condition for the well-functioning of a euro-market centre.
There are no obstacles, either in the form of minimum-reserve requirements or special deposit requirements, or of any other kind;
and there are no maturity constraints on foreign-currency assets
and liabilities, though the maturity structure of euro-operations
of individual banks is supervised and banks are expected, on prudential grounds, to maintain adequate liquidity, and those in-
corporated in the United Kingdom, appropriate capital funds.

(b) <u>Capital inflows via inward switching</u>

Banks are allowed to switch foreign-currency assets into
domestic currency on a covered basis. However, the resulting net
external foreign-currency liabilities are subject to both a minimum
reserve requirement and a variable special deposit requirement,
i.e. minimum ratio requirements that apply to all sterling resources (see section 1 (i) above). The extent to which banks
actually engage in inward switching depends, of course, on the
relevant interest-rate relationships allowing for the cost effects
of the minimum-reserve and the special deposit requirements.

(c) <u>Capital inflows via the use of foreign-currency funds
raised abroad for granting foreign-currency loans to
resident non-banks</u>

With the abolition of the Exchange Control Act 1947 on 23rd
October, 1979, there are now no restrictions on capital inflows to
resident non-banks.

(d) <u>Capital outflows via outward switching</u>

There are no longer any limitations on capital outflows via
banks switching domestic currency into foreign currency assets,
though banks' foreign-currency exposure will be monitored as part
of the process of prudential supervision.

(e) <u>Capital outflows via financing external foreign-currency
assets with foreign-currency deposits from resident
non-banks</u>

No restrictions.

(ii) Commercial banks' domestic-currency operations with non-
    residents

   (f) Domestic-currency liabilities to non-residents

   There are no discriminatory restrictions or disincentives
on non-resident sterling balances held with domestic banks. Interest rates on such accounts are the same as those offered to
resident account holders. Sterling liabilities to non-residents
with an original maturity not exceeding two years and the net
liability to the banks' own overseas offices are subject to the
same minimum reserve and special deposit requirements as sterling
liabilities to residents (See section 1 (i) above).

   (g) Placing domestic-currency funds with foreign banks

   No restrictions.

   (h) Domestic-currency credits and loans to non-resident
       non-banks

   No restrictions.

(iii) Non-bank borrowing and lending operations with non-resident
     banks

   (j) Capital inflows via borrowing from non-resident banks

   No restrictions.

   (k) Capital outflows via placing liquid assets with non-
       resident banks

   No restrictions.

III. SUMMARY VIEW OF REGULATIONS AND INSTRUMENTS AFFECTING INTERNATIONAL BANKING OPERATIONS OF BANKS AND NON-BANKS IN

THE UNITED KINGDOM

(situation at the end of 1980)

Type of Operation or Balance Sheet Position / Type of Regulation or Instrument	Code	I. Exchange Control (1)	II. Minimum Reserve Requirements	III. Interest Rate Control	IV. Prudential Regulations	V. Tax Regulations	VI. Other Regulations or instruments
COMMERCIAL BANKS	1.						
Liability Operations/Positions	11.						
in foreign currencies	11.1						
with non-residents	11.11						
deposits from	11.111						
banks	11.111.1						
non-banks	11.111.2						
credits and loans from	11.112						
banks	11.112.1						
non-banks	11.112.2						
fixed-interest securities	11.113						
money market paper	11.113.1						
bonds	11.113.2						
with residents	11.12						
deposits from	11.121						
banks	11.121.1						
non-banks	11.121.2						
Central Bank or Government	11.121.3						
in domestic currency	11.2						
with non-residents	11.21		x				
current accounts of	11.211						
banks	11.211.1						
non-banks	11.211.2						
time deposits from	11.212						
banks	11.212.1						
non-banks	11.212.2						
credits and loans from	11.213						
banks	11.213.1						
non-banks	11.213.2						
fixed-interest securities	11.214						
money market paper	11.214.1						
bonds	11.214.2						
Asset Operations/Positions	12.						
in foreign currencies	12.1						
with non-residents	12.11						
banks	12.111						
current accounts	12.111.1						
time deposits	12.111.2						
credits and loans	12.111.3						
non-banks	12.112						
credits and loans	12.112.1						
securities	12.113						
with residents	12.12						
deposits with banks	12.121						
credits and loans to non-banks	12.122						
securities	12.123						
deposits with Central bank	12.124						

(1) And similar regulations imposing quantitative controls on capital transactions with non-residents.

(situation at the end of 1980)

Type of Operation or Balance Sheet Position / Type of Regulation or Instrument	Code	I. Exchange Control (1)	II. Minimum Reserve Requirements	III. Interest Rate Control	IV. Prudential Regulations	V. Tax Regulations	VI. Other Regulations or instruments
in domestic currency	12.2						
with non-residents	12.21						
deposits with banks	12.211						
credits and loans to	12.212						
banks	12.212.1						
non-banks	12.212.2						
securities	12.213						
Net Positions	13.						
in foreign currencies	13.1		x				
vis-à-vis non-residents	13.2						
NON-BANKS	2.						
Liability Operations/ Positions	21.						
credits and loans from	21.1						
non-resident banks	21.11						
in foreign currencies	21.111						
in domestic currency	21.112						
resident banks	21.12						
in foreign currencies	21.121						
Asset Operations/Positions	22.						
with non-resident banks	22.1						
in foreign currencies	22.11						
current accounts	22.111						
time deposits	22.112						
in domestic currency	22.12						
deposits	22.121						
with resident banks	22.2						
in foreign currencies	22.21						
current accounts	22.211						
time deposits	22.212						
FOREIGN EXCHANGE OPERATIONS/ POSITIONS	3.						
Commercial Banks	31.						
spot foreign exchange dealings	31.1						
forward foreign exchange dealings	31.2						
swap transactions	31.3						
net foreign exchange positions	31.4				x		
Non-Banks	32.						
spot foreign exchange dealings	32.1				x		
forward foreign exchange dealings	32.2				x		
swap transactions	32.3				x		

(1) And similar regulations imposing quantitative controls on capital transactions with non-residents.

IV. LISTING OF REGULATIONS BY CATEGORIES AND BY
OPERATIONS OR BALANCE SHEET POSITIONS
(situation at the end of 1980)

Code No. of classification schema	Operation/Position	Regulation
	II. MINIMUM RESERVE REQUIREMENTS	
II/11.21	Those commercial banks on the Bank of England's statistical list (1) taking deposits from non-residents (other than their own) overseas offices) in sterling with an original maturity of two years or under; (2) having a net sterling liability, regardless of term to maturity, to their own overseas offices;	) Liabilities arising) under the operational) positions listed op-) posite are included) in the calculation of) a bank's total eli-) gible liabilities) (see section 1(i))) which were subject to) 12.5 per cent minimum) reserve requirements,) i.e. an equivalent of
II/13.1	(3) having net foreign-currency) liabilities, i.e. that part of foreign-currency resources that is switched into sterling resources (inward switching).	) 12.5 per cent of such) liabilities was to be) held in specified re-) serve assets (general-) ly liquid assets); in) addition, subject to) the requirements of) special deposits with) the Bank of England,) the minimum reserve) requirement was re-) duced to 10 per cent) with effect from 5th) January 1981.

Code No. of classification schema	Operation/Position	Regulation
	IV. PRUDENTIAL REGULATIONS	
IV.31/4	Net Foreign exchange positions) of commercial banks))))))	There are no restrictions on Foreign currency dealings by banks but their Foreign currency exposure is subject to prudential surveillance.
IV.32.1	Spot Foreign exchange dealings) by non-banks))	There are no restrictions on Foreign currency dealings by non-banks but the Foreign currency exposure of deposit-taking institutions is subject to prudential surveillance.
IV.32.2	Forward Foreign exchange dealings by non-banks))	
IV.32.3	Swap transactions by non-banks))))	

V. PRINCIPAL SOURCES OF LEGAL AND REGULATORY PROVISIONS

Minimum-Reserve Requirements

"Competition and credit control" which came into force in September 1971; from time to time variations to the original scheme have been made.

Prudential Regulations

Banking Act 1979.

Annex I

I. NOTES ON TERMINOLOGY, DEFINITIONS AND CONCEPTS

A. INTERNATIONAL BANKING OPERATIONS: CONCEPTS OF ANALYSIS

1. Introduction

The term "international banking operations" as used in the present publication covers two broad areas of international banking which today are both of considerable importance:

a) euro-banking - or euro-market - business which largely, but not exclusively, consists of foreign-currency denominated asset and liability operations of banks located in a given country with banks and non-banks located inside and outside the same country (example: banks located in the United Kingdom accept dollar deposits from non-resident or resident banks and non-banks or grant dollar loans to non-resident or resident banks or non-banks);

b) traditional foreign banking business which largely, but not exclusively, consists of domestic-currency denominated asset and liability operations of banks located in a given country with banks and non-banks located in other countries (example: banks located in the United States accept dollar deposits from non-residents or grant dollar loans to non-residents).

These two more commonly used terms - "euro-market operations" and "traditional foreign banking operations" - have been avoided in the classification of international banking operations given in the synoptic table of Section III of each country note. The reason for this is that these terms are generally not used in banking regulations because they are rather complicated to define as will be shown further below; and because these distinctions are rarely considered meaningful from the point of view of banking control. The currency denomination for a given international banking operation, that is, whether it is carried out in domestic currency or in foreign currency, is from a regulation point of view frequently considered as a more essential criterion. Therefore, this latter distinction between domestic- and foreign-currency operations has been applied not only in Sections III and IV but also in Section II of each country note (Analysis of regulations by main types of capital movements) which contains three sub-sections:

i) commercial banks' foreign-currency operations;
ii) commercial banks' domestic-currency operations with non-residents;
iii) non-bank borrowing and lending operations with non-resident banks (covering both domestic- and foreign-currency operations).[1]

However, from the point of view of financial market analysis, the above-mentioned distinction between euro-market operations and traditional foreign banking operations seems important enough to justify a detailed explanation and clarification of these terms which may facilitate the understanding of how and to what extent the regulations described in the country notes are related, and relevant, to the euro-market and its functioning.

In the following paragraphs, after briefly explaining the differences between euro-market operations and foreign-currency operations on the one hand, and between traditional foreign banking operations and domestic-currency operations on the other, an attempt is made to bring out the characteristic features of the two categories of international banking operations by commented schemas (see Appendix to this note) which are at the same time intended as a methodological guide to classifying and analysing individual countries with regard to their respective roles in the field of international banking. In addition, there are more detailed comments on the classification of international banking operations according to their balance-of-payments effects which is applied in Section II of each country note.

2. Euro-market operations and foreign-currency operations[2]

Euro-market operations are not identical with foreign-currency operations though for lack of better data the volume of euro-market operations is generally measured by data on foreign-currency assets and liabilities of commercial banks and though euro-market operations actually consist largely of foreign-currency denominated asset and liability operations. However, there are the following exceptions with some of them playing an important role:

a) the following foreign-currency operations fall outside the scope of the euro-market and belong to the area of traditional foreign banking operations:

1. Non-bank borrowing and lending operations with non-resident banks are included in the analysis of international banking operations because one contracting party is a bank and because it is important to know in this context to what extent and under which conditions non-banks located in a given country may carry out operations with banks located in other countries.

2. See also note b) of this Annex on "Terminology, definitions and concepts relating to the euro-market".

118

i) banks or non-banks acquiring foreign-exchange balances in the foreign-exchange markets; by doing so the banks or non-banks register an increase in foreign-currency claims on a bank located in the country of issue of the currency in question;

ii) banks or non-banks investing funds in national money markets of other countries; by doing so the banks or non-banks acquire interest-bearing claims issued by banks or other bodies in a given country which are denominated in that country's currency (example: banks or non-banks in Germany acquiring dollar certificates of deposit of banks located in the United States);

iii) banks or non-banks raising foreign-currency loans from banks located in a country whose currency is used (example: a bank in the United Kingdom using its overdraft facility on its current dollar account held with its correspondent bank located in the United States).

It should be noted that the three items mentioned are, with regard to the currency used, asymmetric in the sense that the operations involve a foreign-currency for only one contracting party, the other party operating in its own domestic currency. This is illustrated in Chart B by items I. i)a) and b), and III. ii); the counterparts of these trans- actions are found in Chart D as items I. ii) and III. i) and ii). In addition, there may be certain foreign-currency denominated operations between banks and non-banks of one and the same country, notably in connection with trade financing, which should be considered as traditional banking operations and not as euro-market operations (see items II. i) and ii) of Chart B);

b)   the following domestic-currency operations fall into the category of euro-market operations:

i) banks or non-banks located in a country whose currency is actively used as a euro-currency investing domestic-currency funds in a foreign euro-market centre (example: banks or non-banks located in Germany placing Deutsche Mark deposits with banks in the United Kingdom);

ii) banks or non-banks located in a country whose currency is actively used as a euro-currency borrowing domestic-currency funds from a foreign euro-market centre (example: banks or non-banks located in Germany raising euro-DM loans from banks located in Luxembourg).

These two items are, with regard to the currency use, also asym- metric in the sense that a foreign currency is involved for only one contracting party, the other party operating in its own domestic currency. This is illustrated in Chart C by items I. iv) and III. iv);

119

the counterparts of these transactions are found in the same Chart C
as items I. iii) and III. iii).

3. Traditional foreign banking operations and domestic-currency
    operations

Though the bulk of traditional foreign banking business consists of
domestic-currency denominated asset and liability operations of banks
located in the country whose currency is used, with banks or non-banks
located in other countries, important additions and subtractions have to
be made in order to arrive at an adequate list of traditional foreign
banking operations; in fact, the three types of foreign-currency operations listed in Section 2. above, namely the acquisition of foreign
exchange, investments in national money markets of other countries
and borrowing from national financial systems of other countries in
those countries' domestic currencies, have to be added; and accordingly,
the two types of domestic-currency operations mentioned in the same
Section, namely investment or raising of domestic-currency funds in
foreign euro-market centres, have to be subtracted.

4. Essential characteristics of euro-market operations and of tradi-
    tional foreign banking operations

The preceding comparison of euro-market operations and foreign-
currency operations on the one hand and traditional foreign banking
operations and domestic-currency operations on the other, has made
it clear that the currency criterion cannot be entirely relied on in
distinguishing conceptually as well as statistically between euro-market
operations and traditional foreign banking operations. Even in cases
where banks in Europe, for example, report dollar claims on the
United States, it is not clear without additional information whether
the underlying transaction represents a euro-market operation or a
traditional foreign banking operation; if the claims consist of foreign
exchange (i. e. current account dollar balances held with banks located
in the United States), U.S. money market instruments or time deposits,
the operation is to be classified as a traditional foreign banking operation. If, however, the claims arise from U.S. banks or non-banks
borrowing actively in the euro-dollar market at euro-dollar market
interest rates it is clear that the operation has to be classified as a
euro-market operation. Thus, it would seem that, speaking in ana-
lytical and not in statistical terms,* the only meaningful criterion for

---

* Statistics on commercial banks foreign-currency claims on, and liabilities to,
non-residents and residents; and on domestic-currency claims on, and liabilities to, non-
residents, which are published by the Bank for International Settlements and a number of
central banks do, under present conditions, not allow to distinguish between euro-market
operations proper and other international banking operations. However, the Bank for International Settlements makes attempts at estimating the size of the euro-market according
to the definitions of euro-market operations which are given in this note and note B of this
Annex.

distinguishing between euro-market operations and traditional foreign banking operations is the interest rate which is paid or earned on a given transaction; euro-market operations are remunerated at interest rates which are freely and flexibly determined by demand and supply in the most important centre of the euro-market, the London interbank market, or which are closely related to London interbank market rates whilst traditional foreign banking operations are remunerated at interest rates which are essentially determined in the domestic financial markets of the countries whose currencies are used. This does not exclude, of course, that in specific market areas there is a close relationship between interest rates paid on euro-market operations and those paid on traditional foreign banking operations denominated in the same currency.

The charts and comments presented in the Appendix to this note give, in schematical form, more detail on the characteristics of euro-market operations and traditional foreign banking operations as seen from the point of view of an individual country, and with a distinction being made between countries which function as financial centres either for euro-market operations or traditional foreign banking operations and countries which have only borrowing and lending links with such centres without being financial centres themselves.

5.   Classification of international banking operations according to their balance-of-payments effects

In practice, countries involved in international banking operations as borrowers, lenders or intermediaries (financial centres) may combine features of several of the five schemas presented in Charts A to E of the Appendix. However, whilst such distinctions between euro-market operations and traditional foreign banking operations are important for the analysis of financial markets and related interest-rate developments, it should be noted that from the point of view of an individual country's policies regarding international banking operations, the authorities are usually more concerned with balance-of-payments and exchange-rate effects of such transactions irrespective of whether they represent euro-market operations or traditional foreign banking operations. For this reason, as has already been mentioned earlier, the distinction between two categories of international banking operations has not been made in the country notes. Rather, it has been considered more important to classify international banking operations - apart from distinguishing between foreign-currency and domestic-currency operations - by types of capital movements and to examine how such capital flows are affected by various categories of regulations. Such is the purpose of Section II in each country note.

The first question examined (see Section II. item i) a)) is to what extent and under which conditions banks located in the country concerned are permitted to function as intermediaries between borrowers and lenders located in foreign countries, i. e. to carry out what is sometimes called "entrepôt" or "turntable" business in foreign currencies. This type of business is neutral from the point of view of the country's balance of payments and exchange rate.

The next two items deal with capital inflows which may arise from foreign-currency business of the banking sector. Banks raising foreign-currency funds abroad by active borrowing or by accepting deposits may use the proceeds for domestic purposes in two ways:

- either by switching the foreign currency into domestic currency (Section II, item i) b)), or

- by granting foreign-currency loans to resident firms or the public sector (Section II, item i) c)).

The latter form of capital inflow is sometimes chosen for exchange-cover reasons; however, the first type of operation - inward switching - usually has also to be carried out on a covered basis, i. e. in the form of a swap operation (a combination of a spot sale of foreign currency and a forward repurchase of the same amount of foreign currency against domestic currency).

Subsequently, two forms of capital outflow are examined:

- capital outflows via outward switching, i. e. by acquiring foreign currency against domestic currency for employment abroad which usually has to be done on a covered basis, as in the case of inward switching (Section II, item i) d));

- matching foreign-currency deposits from residents with foreign-currency claims on non-residents (Section II, item i) e)).

The next sub-section (see Section II, item ii) f), g), h)) deals with three types of capital flows which may arise in connection with commercial banks' domestic-currency operations with non-residents:

- movements in domestic-currency liabilities of commercial banks to non-residents with an increase in such liabilities being registered in the balance-of-payments as a capital inflow, and a decrease as a capital outflow;

- a capital outflow produced by commercial banks placing domestic-currency funds with banks abroad (earning euro-market rates); this applies only to countries whose currencies are actively used as euro-currencies;

- a capital outflow representing domestic-currency credits and loans to non-residents (earning domestic interest rates).

In some country cases such as Germany and Switzerland it has been necessary to deal also with the question of capital inflows via foreign purchases of domestic-currency denominated fixed-interest securities, though such transactions are, in the context of the present study, not considered as international banking transactions proper; measures in this area are sometimes taken in order to prevent circumvention or restrictions affecting inflows of foreign capital via domestic-currency banking accounts.

The final sub-section (see Section II, item iii j) and k)) deals with borrowing and lending operations of non-banks located in a given country with banks located in another country addressing the questions to what extent and under which conditions are non-banks allowed to borrow from banks in other countries in foreign or domestic currency and to what extent and under which conditions are they allowed to hold and place liquid funds - in foreign or domestic currency - with banks abroad. Other capital operations of the non-banking sector are not examined as the scope of the study is limited to international banking operations.

It has not been found necessary to deal with those capital operations which simply represent a reversal of the operations described, such as repatriation of foreign assets or withdrawals of foreign deposits held with domestic banks, such operations being free in all countries examined.

The classification of international banking operations according to types of capital movements is summarised in the following schema:

Simplified Schema of Analysis of International Flows of Banking Funds*

I.   TRANSIT-FLOWS

Banks functioning as international intermediaries
and borrowing foreign-currency funds abroad for relending
abroad (international "entrepot" or "turntable" business)

II. CAPITAL OUTFLOWS	III. CAPITAL INFLOWS
(i) Banks lending funds to non-residents on the basis of domestic sources:	(i) Banks borrowing funds from non-residents for domestic use**:
a) increase in foreign-currency assets	a) increase in foreign-currency liabilities
1) financed via outward switching (i. e. via converting domestic currency on the foreign exchange market)	1) for domestic use via inward switching (foreign-currency proceeds converted on the foreign-exchange market against domestic currency)
2) financed with foreign-currency deposits from residents non-banks	2) for domestic use via foreign-currency loans to resident non-banks
b) increase in domestic-currency assets	b) increase in domestic-currency liabilities
(ii) Non-banks lending funds to banks abroad (in the form to foreign- or domestic-currency deposits)	(ii) Non-banks borrowing funds from banks abroad (in foreign or domestic currency)

---

* Applying to an individual country and covering capital flows between banks located
inside the country and banks abroad (international interbank operations) and between
banks and non-banks of different countries.

** It should be noted that only first-step uses are considered in this schema. In practice,
capital imports via inward switching operations or via foreign-currency loans granted
to resident non-banks (item III. (i) a)1) and 2)) may ultimately be used externally,
for example for the financing of imports of goods and services; however, such second-
step uses are not taken into account, a principle which applies to balance-of-payments
accounting generally.

APPENDIX

Chart A

SCHEMA OF EURO-MARKET OPERATIONS OF AN INDIVIDUAL COUNTRY
OTHER THAN A EURO-MARKET CENTRE *

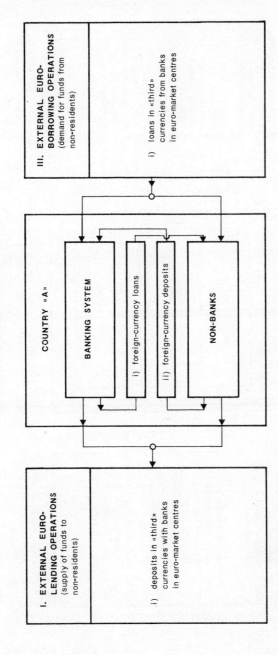

COUNTRY «A»

BANKING SYSTEM

i) foreign-currency loans

ii) foreign-currency deposits

NON-BANKS

I. EXTERNAL EURO-
LENDING OPERATIONS
(supply of funds to
non-residents)

i) deposits in «third»
currencies with banks
in euro-market centres

III. EXTERNAL EURO-
BORROWING OPERATIONS
(demand for funds from
non-residents)

i) loans in «third»
currencies from banks
in euro-market centres

* and whose currency is not used as a euro-currency.

NOTE: Chart A presents a schema of euro-market operations of an individual country other than a euro-market centre country and whose currency is not used as a euro-currency. Such a country's relations with the euro-banking market consist of borrowing and lending operations with banks in a euro-market centre country which are carried out in "third" currencies i.e. currencies which are neither the debtor nor the borrower country's currency (example: banks or non-banks in Mexico borrowing US dollars from, or depositing US dollars with, banks in London).

Chart B

SCHEMA OF «TRADITIONAL» FOREIGN FINANCIAL OPERATIONS OF AN INDIVIDUAL COUNTRY OTHER THAN A FINANCIAL CENTRE COUNTRY*

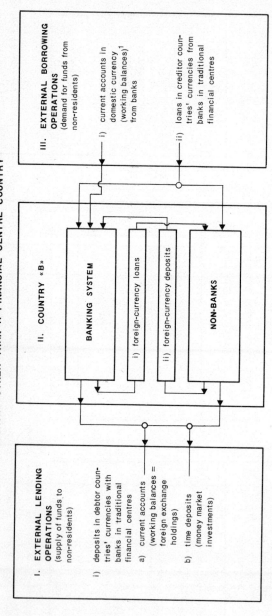

I. EXTERNAL LENDING OPERATIONS
(supply of funds to non-residents)

i) deposits in debtor countries' currencies with banks in traditional financial centres

  a) current accounts (working balances = foreign exchange holdings)

  b) time deposits (money market investments)

II. COUNTRY «B»

BANKING SYSTEM

i) foreign-currency loans

ii) foreign-currency deposits

NON-BANKS

III. EXTERNAL BORROWING OPERATIONS
(demand for funds from non-residents)

i) current accounts in domestic currency (working balances)[1] from banks

ii) loans in creditor countries' currencies from banks in traditional financial centres

* and whose currencies are not actively used for effecting international payments.

1. representing foreign exchange holdings from the foreign holders point of view ; even if the currency is not actively used for international payments foreign commercial banks need to hold certain amounts of working balances for foreign exchange dealings.

NOTE: Chart B, by contrast, shows, is schematical form, traditional foreign banking operations of an individual country other than a financial centre country. Such a country's traditional foreign banking links consist of foreign-exchange holdings (clearing-account balances) and money market investments in traditional financial centres and liabilities to banks in such centres ; the currency which is used is that of the financial centre country in which the foreign-exchange reserves are held or from which funds are borrowed (example: banks or non-banks borrowing dollars from, or holding dollars with, banks in the United States). In practice, most countries which do not perform a role as international financial centres have international banking links which are a combination of the ones shown in Charts A and B.

126

Chart C

SCHEMA OF EURO-MARKET OPERATIONS OF AN INDIVIDUAL COUNTRY FUNCTIONING AS A EURO-MARKET CENTRE*

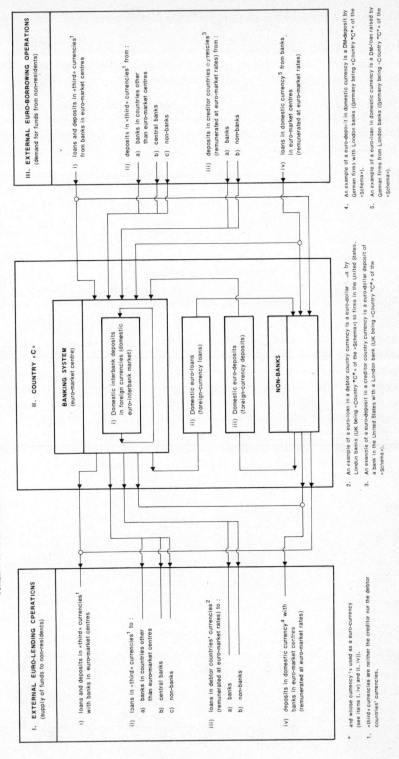

I. EXTERNAL EURO-LENDING OPERATIONS
(supply of funds to non-residents)

i) loans and deposits in «third» currencies[1] with banks in euro-market centres

ii) loans in «third» currencies[1] to :
   a) banks in countries other than euro-market centres
   b) central banks
   c) non-banks

iii) loans in debtor countries' currencies[2] (remunerated at euro-market rates) to :
   a) banks
   b) non-banks

iv) deposits in domestic currency[4] with banks in euro-market centres (remunerated at euro-market rates)

II. COUNTRY «C»

BANKING SYSTEM
(euro-market centre)

i) Domestic interbank deposits in foreign currencies (domestic euro-interbank market)

ii) Domestic euro-loans (foreign-currency loans)

iii) Domestic euro-deposits (foreign-currency deposits)

NON-BANKS

III. EXTERNAL EURO-BORROWING OPERATIONS
(demand for funds from non-residents)

i) loans and deposits in «third» currencies[1] from banks in euro-market centres

ii) deposits in «third» currencies[1] from :
   a) banks in countries other than euro-market centres
   b) central banks
   c) non-banks

iii) deposits in creditor countries' currencies[3] (remunerated at euro-market rates) from :
   a) banks
   b) non-banks

iv) loans in domestic currency[5] from banks in euro-market centres (remunerated at euro-market rates)

* and whose currency is used as a euro-currency (see items I. iv) and II. iv)).

1. «third» currencies are neither the creditor nor the debtor countries' currencies.

2. An example of a euro-loan in a debtor country currency is a euro-dollar ...n by London banks (UK being «Country "C"» of the «Schema») to firms in the United States.

3. An example of a euro-deposit in a creditor country currency is a euro-dollar deposit of a bank in the United States with a London bank (UK being «Country "C"» of the «Schema»).

4. An example of a euro-deposit in domestic currency is a DM-deposit by German firms with London banks (Germany being «Country "C"» of the «Schema»).

5. An example of a euro-loan in domestic currency is a DM-loan raised by German firms from London banks (Germany being «Country "C"» of the «Schema»).

Note to Chart C:

Chart C contains a schema of euro-market operations of an individual country functioning as a euro-market centre. Using the currency aspect as a criterion for classification, three
categories of borrowing and lending operations may be distinguished:

(a) operations in a "third" currency, i.e. in a currency which is neither the lender nor
the borrower country's currency with banks (including central banks) and non-banks in other
countries (items I.i) and ii), III.i) and ii)) and with banks and non-banks inside the country
(items II.i), ii) and iii));

(b) loans in debtor countries' currencies and deposits in creditor countries remunerated
at euro-market rates (items I.iii) and III.iii)) (example: banks in the United Kingdom
granting US dollar loans to non-banks in the United States or taking euro-dollar deposits
from non-banks in the United States);

(c) deposits with, and loans from, banks in other euro-market centres in domestic
currency remunerated at euro-market rates (items I.iv) and III.iv)) (example: banks or
non-banks in Germany placing Deutsche Mark deposits with, or raising Deutsche Mark funds
from, banks in Luxembourg with Germany being Country C of the schema). This case can
only apply to euro-market centre countries whose currencies are actively used as euro-
currencies.

The schema confirms what has been said earlier, namely that the currency criterion cannot
be used throughout to distinguish statistically between euro-banking operations and traditional
foreign banking operations; for example, a US dollar claim of a bank in the United Kingdom
on a bank in the United States can represent a time deposit remunerated at rates prevailing
in the United States (traditional banking operations: see Chart D, item I.i) b)) or a euro-
dollar loan remunerated at euro-market rates (euro-banking operation: see Chart C, item
I.iii) a)). The essential criterion for identifying euro-market operations is thus the interest
rate which is applied. Statistics on external claims and liabilities of bank which are available
today do not, however, allow the taking into account of such refined distinctions.

Chart D

SCHEMA OF «TRADITIONAL» FOREIGN FINANCIAL OPERATIONS OF AN INDIVIDUAL COUNTRY FUNCTIONING AS A «TRADITIONAL» FINANCIAL CENTRE*

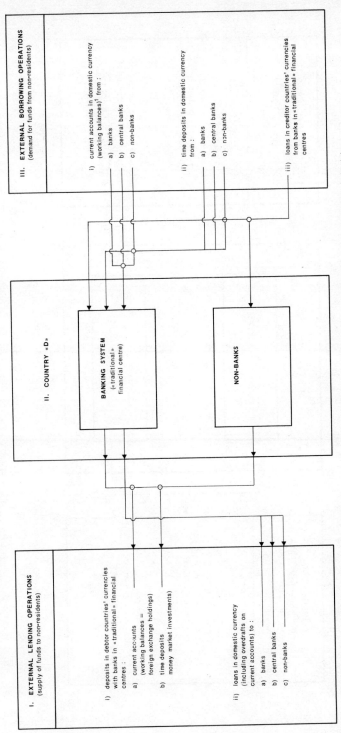

I. EXTERNAL LENDING OPERATIONS
(supply of funds to non-residents)

i) deposits in debtor countries' currencies with banks in «traditional» financial centres :

a) current accounts (working balances = foreign exchange holdings)

b) time deposits money market investments)

ii) loans in domestic currency (including overdrafts on current accounts) to :

a) banks
b) central banks
c) non-banks

II. COUNTRY «D»

BANKING SYSTEM
(«traditional» financial centre)

NON-BANKS

III. EXTERNAL BORROWING OPERATIONS
(demand for funds from non-residents)

i) current accounts in domestic currency (working balances)[1] from :

a) banks
b) central banks
c) non-banks

ii) time deposits in domestic currency from :

a) banks
b) central banks
c) non-banks

iii) loans in creditor countries' currencies from banks in «traditional» financial centres

* and whose currency is actively used for effecting international payments.

NOTE: Chart D presents a schema of traditional foreign banking operations of an individual country functioning as a traditional financial centre. It is characteristic of such operations that they are denominated in the centre country's own domestic currency and carry domestically determined interest rates. The country may have traditional foreign banking links with other countries functioning as traditional financial centres, which is indicated in the Chart by items I. i)a) and b) and III. iii).

1. representing foreign exchange holdings from the foreign holders' point of view.

129

Chart E

SCHEMA OF EURO-MARKET OPERATIONS OF AN INDIVIDUAL COUNTRY FUNCTIONING AS A «TRADITIONAL» FINANCIAL CENTRE*

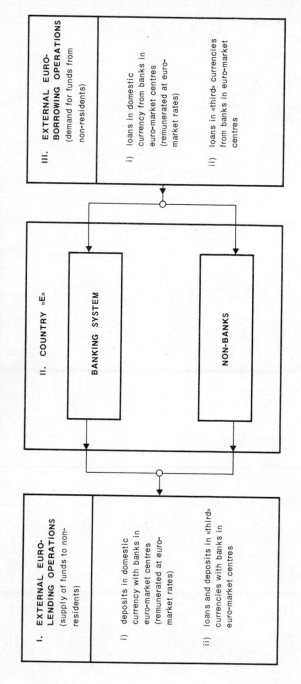

I. EXTERNAL EURO-LENDING OPERATIONS (supply of funds to non-residents)

i) deposits in domestic currency with banks in euro-market centres (remunerated at euro-market rates)

ii) loans and deposits in «third» currencies with banks in euro-market centres

II. COUNTRY «E»

BANKING SYSTEM

NON-BANKS

III. EXTERNAL EURO-BORROWING OPERATIONS (demand for funds from non-residents)

i) loans in domestic currency from banks in euro-market centres (remunerated at euro-market rates)

ii) loans in «third» currencies from banks in euro-market centres

* and whose currency is used as a euro-currency.

NOTE: Chart E, finally, shows in schematical form euro-market operations of a country which functions as a traditional financial centre but not as a euro-market centre though its currency is actively used as a euro-currency. Euro-market links are in this case likely to be largely confined to domestic-currency borrowing and lending operations with banks in euro-market centres. In addition, there may be borrowing and lending operations denominated in "third" currencies i.e. in currencies which are neither the borrowing nor the lending countries' currencies.

130

B. TERMINOLOGY, DEFINITIONS AND CONCEPTS RELATING TO THE EURO-MARKET

1. General

In the context of this study, the term <u>euro-market</u> is used as a short synonym for the terms <u>euro-currency market</u> or <u>euro-money market</u>; the <u>euro-bond market</u> is not meant to be covered, though in practice there is a certain degree of interpenetration of these two market areas with corresponding relatively close interest-rate inter-relationships.

The euro-market in this delineation is a combination of an international money market for short- and medium-term interbank and non-banking funds and an international short- and medium-term bank credit market; it has a number of special characteristics as regards the participants, the amounts involved in single transactions, the formation of interest rates, and the currency denomination which is applied.

One contracting party in a single euro-market operation, either the creditor or the debtor, is always a bank, disregarding certain secondary market transactions between non-banks in marketable euro-money market paper such as euro-dollar certificates of deposit (CDs) or euro-commercial paper. The other party is frequently another bank (euro-interbank-market transactions), but may also be a central bank, a government body, an industrial and commercial enterprise, an international organisation, an institutional investor or a wealthy individual. Small savers are generally excluded as participants. Most transactions are between residents of different countries (international capital transactions). However, in certain countries with important euro-market centres euro-market transactions between residents of that country play a relatively important role. The amounts involved in single transactions are generally large, i. e. mostly not smaller than one million currency units, which by itself is a limiting factor with regard to the number and categories of market participants ("wholesale market").

Interest rates in all market areas are flexible and closely inter-related with the base rates of the market which are freely determined, under highly competitive conditions, by demand and supply forces prevailing in the interbank market - essentially the London interbank market which is the largest local market of this kind; in other words, there are generally no interest-rate cartel agreements between participating banks nor are interest rates regulated by governments or central banks though the latter may influence rates by measures affecting demand and supply conditions in the market.

Euro-market assets and liabilities are frequently denominated in a "third" currency, i. e. a currency which is neither the debtor country's nor the creditor country's currency. However, residents of some of those countries whose currencies are actively used as euro-currencies, notably residents of the United States, Germany, Switzerland and the Netherlands may also engage in euro-market operations which are denominated in their own domestic currency.

For more detail on the question of the currency denomination of euro-market operations: see in the present Annex I the note on "International Banking Operations: Concepts of Analysis", sub-section 2. and Chart C of the Appendix to that note.

2.   The concept of a euro-market centre (i. e. of an individual country's euro-market system) and the statistical measurement of its size

The term euro-market centre refers to a country whose banking system plays a role as an intermediary of euro-market funds, which is important in relation to the euro-market as a whole (consisting of all individual euro-market centres) and also in relation to total banking activity in that country. The operators of an individual euro-market centre are the commercial banks located in that country; they may be domestic (i. e. resident-owned) banks or foreign-owned branches and subsidiaries. Domestic banks' foreign branches and subsidiaries (operating in other countries) are not considered as forming part of the banking system of the country in question. That part of an individual country's banking system which is engaged in euro-market operations may also be referred to as the country's euro-market system.

The statistical measurement of the size of an individual country's euro-market system (euro-market centre) poses a number of conceptual and statistical problems. From the point of view of data availability the most promising approach, under present circumstances, is to apply the schema on the following page:

This schema is only an approximation for measuring the size of a euro-market centre; data compiled accordingly would not provide a fully adequate picture of the euro-market activities of an individual country's banking system because - as has already been explained in the note on "International Banking Operations: Concepts of analysis" (sub-section 2.) - certain categories of foreign-currency assets[1] and

1.   For example, foreign-exchange holdings, investments in other countries' domestic money markets, holdings of foreign-currency denominated securities and trade bills.

Schema for measuring the size
of an individual country's euro-market system[*]

(assets and liabilities of commercial banks:
outstanding amounts at the end of period)[1]

USES	SOURCES
1. Euro-claims on residents foreign-currency claims on a) banks b) non-banks	1. Euro-liabilities to residents foreign-currency liabilities to a) banks b) non-banks
2. Euro-claims on non-residents a) banks b) non-banks	2. Euro-liabilities to non-residents a) banks b) non-banks
3. Other uses, net (balancing item applying if identified euro-claims are smaller than identified euro-liabilities)	3. Other sources, net (balancing item applying if identified euro-claims exceed identified euro-liabilities)
4. Total euro-market uses =	4. Total euro-market sources

1. The schema can also be applied to flow data.

* Measuring the size of an individual country's euro-market as the sum of all identified euro-liabilities, or euro-assets, whichever side of the balance-sheet is larger, and introducing "other uses (net)" or "other sources (net)" as a balancing item, raises conceptual problems insofar as this method tends to underestimate the "true" flow-of-funds channelled through the euro-market of the country in question. The reason for this is that some individual banks may report "other uses (net)" while others may report "other sources (net)" as balancing items which will be netted out as a result of aggregation so that for the banking system as a whole one single balancing item remains. Even in the case of one single bank, it is conceivable that individual euro-market operations move in opposite directions so that, on a gross basis, the bank in question would have to report both certain euro-liabilities matched by "other uses" and certain euro-claims matched by "other sources". Thus, the suggested method of measuring the size of an individual country's euro-market has to be considered as giving approximate results.

liabilities[2] of a country's banking system do not belong to the euro-market area.

Moreover, the schema does not allow the inclusion of certain euro-market assets and liabilities which, in the case of some countries whose currencies are actively used in the euro-market, may be denominated in domestic currencies. The main reason for excluding such domestic-currency denominated euro-claims and euro-liabilities is the fact that under present circumstances such items, statistically speaking, are difficult to distinguish from other domestic-currency claims and liabilities which belong to the sphere of "traditional" foreign banking, as the interest rate would be the essential criterion for such a distinction. *

In measuring the size of an individual country's euro-market system a distinction may be made between the gross size and the net size of the system. Leaving aside the problems of inadequacy of statistics just mentioned, the item "total euro-market uses" (or "total euro-market sources") of the schema would provide a measure of the "gross size" of the system; whilst the "net size" would be obtained by deducting domestic interbank claims and liabilities (item 1. a) on both the uses and sources side) from the total. The exclusion of domestic interbank claims and liabilities in foreign currencies could be justified by the argument that from the point of view of the banking system as a whole these items do not represent outside uses and sources in the sense that domestic interbank operations leave the system's liquid resources unchanged while all other euro-market operations listed lead to inflows of funds into, or outflows of funds from, the system.

3. The concept of the euro-market system as a whole and the statistical measurement of its size

Speaking conceptually, and not statistically, the euro-market system as a whole would comprise all assets and liabilities of commercial banks which are remunerated at euro-market interest rates;

2. For example, drawing on credit lines provided by foreign correspondent banks, issues of bankers acceptances in connection with trade financing, issues of foreign-currency notes and bonds.

* Statistics on commercial banks foreign-currency claims on, and liabilities to, non-residents and residents; and on domestic-currency claims on, and liabilities to, non-residents, which are published by the Bank for International Settlements and a number of central banks do, under present conditions, not allow to distinguish between euro-market operations proper and other international banking operations. However, the Bank for International Settlements makes attempts at estimating the size of the euro-market according to the definitions of euro-market operations which are given in this note and note B of this Annex.

134

in this sense, the euro-market concept is one relating to specific categories of financial instruments rather than to a specific type of financial institution. A statistical measure of the size of the euro-market as a whole would be obtained by aggregating the data on euro-market claims and liabilities of the banking systems of individual countries which play a role as euro-market centres. As in the case of an individual country's euro-market system, a distinction could be made between the gross and the net size of the system as a whole: the gross-size would be the sum of total euro-market sources (uses) of the individual euro-market centres, and the net size would be obtained by netting out all euro-interbank claims (liabilities) inside the system, which, from the point of view of the system taken as a whole, represent no original sources or ultimate uses of funds.

As is illustrated by Chart F, ultimate uses of system funds consist of euro-loans to all borrowers in the "outside area", to non-banks inside the euro-market area (all reporting countries taken together) and to the national banking systems inside the euro-market area. Correspondingly, original sources of system funds consist of all flows (remunerated at euro-market rates) received from the "outside area", from non-banks inside the area and from national banking systems inside the area.[3]

The concept of ultimate uses and original sources of the euro-market system as a whole, just briefly discussed, is important for purposes of market analysis; however, from the point of view of an individual country's policy, all euro-market transactions with other countries are relevant whether representing "intra-system" flows or ultimate uses or original sources of euro-market funds.

C.   GLOSSARY RELATING TO INTERNATIONAL BANKING OPERATIONS

The term "banking" operations refers to interbank operations (from bank to bank) as well as to operations between banks and non-banks, or banks and central banks.

The terms "banks" and "commercial banks" are used as synonyms and are meant to exclude central banks and specialised credit intitutions.* Accordingly, the term "non-bank" is meant to comprise non financial enterprises as well as financial institutions other than commercial banks.

3.   Available statistics do not normally allow the identification directly, of flows of funds between the euro-market system and national banking systems inside the reporting area as such flows essentially arise in connection with inward or outward switching operations. Such flows may, however, be measured indirectly as the difference between identified euro-assets and euro-liabilities of the banking system of each individual reporting country (see items 3 on the uses and the sources side of the "Schema for measuring the size of an individual country's euro-market system").

*   It should be noted that within the framework of "euro-currency market" statistics such as published by the Bank for International Settlements the term "banks" covers both "commercial banks" and "central banks".

SCHEMA OF USES AND SOURCES OF THE EURO-MARKET SYSTEM AS A WHOLE

«OUTSIDE» AREA

EURO-MARKET AREA

National banking systems
(incl. central banks)

EURO-MARKET SYSTEM
(reporting commercial banks)

SOURCES

USES

Intra-System

Uses   Sources

Central
banks

Commercial
banks

Non-banks

Central
banks

Commercial
banks

Non-banks

Non-banks

EURO-MARKET AREA

«OUTSIDE» SREA

The term "international" in principle refers to transactions or relations between residents and non-residents, i. e. between economic agents such as banks, government bodies, non-financial enterprises, etc. located in different countries. However, in the context of this study certain transactions between residents of one and the same country are also considered as international transactions insofar as they are usually closely connected with transactions between residents and non-residents. This applies notably to foreign-currency transactions between residents, i. e. either foreign-exchange dealings or credit operations between residents, with claims (or debts) being denominated in a foreign currency. Credit operations between residents and non-residents give rise to the creation of "external" or "foreign" claims or liabilities. From the point of view of an individual country, such external (=foreign) claims may be denominated in foreign currencies (=external foreign-currency claims or debts) or in domestic currency (=external domestic-currency claims or debts). External claims or liabilities may also be referred to as claims on, or liabilities to, non-residents. The term "non-resident deposits" means external deposits or deposits owned by non-residents.

Attention should be paid to the use of the term "foreign banks". In the context of the present study a distinction is made between banks located in different countries, irrespective of ownership relations, whether such banks are owned by nationals of the respective country or whether they are foreign-owned. Banks located inside a given country are sometimes referred to as domestic or resident banks (which include foreign-owned banks located in the respective country); and banks located outside a given country are sometimes referred to as foreign or non-resident banks, or banks abroad.

D. GLOSSARY RELATING TO FOREIGN-EXCHANGE MARKETS AND OPERATIONS

The term "foreign exchange" refers to international means of payments which are traded in the "foreign-exchange markets"; leaving aside coins and bank notes, "foreign exchange" consists of current-account, or clearing account, balances (sight deposits) held with banks in the country of issue of a given currency, which can be used for effecting international payments by means of cheques or telegraphic (or other) transfers.

Foreign-exchange balances are reported as external foreign-currency claims as far as the holders are concerned; and as external domestic-currency liabilities as far as the banks are concerned with which the foreign-exchange balances are held.

A distinction is made between "spot transactions" (usually two days delivery) and "forward transactions" (more than two days delivery: 7 days, 1 month, 3 months, etc.); claims and liabilities arising in connection with forward-exchange operations are not usually reported

Chart G

SCHEMA OF RELATIONSHIPS BETWEEN EXTERNAL POSITION, OVERALL FOREIGN-EXCHANGE POSITION, AND EURO-MARKET POSITION OF AN INDIVIDUAL COUNTRY'S BANKING SYSTEM

BANKING SYSTEM

ASSETS	LIABILITIES
1. Domestic-currency claims on non-residents [1]	1. Domestic-currency debts vis-à-vis non-residents [1]
2. Foreign-currency claims (other than Euromarket claims) on non-residents	2. Foreign-currency debts (other than Euro-market debts) vis-à-vis non-residents
3. Euro-market claims on non-residents	3. Euro-market debts vis-à-vis non-residents
4. Euro-market claims on residents	4. Euro-market debts vis-à-vis residents
5. Forward foreign-exchange claims [2]	5. Forward foreign-exchange liabilities [2]

EXTERNAL POSITION

FOREIGN EXCHANGE POSITION

EURO-MARKET POSITION

1. In the case of countries whose currencies are used as euro-currencies, this item may include domestic-currency claims on (or liabilities to) banks in other euro-market centres, which should be added to the euro-market position.

2. Not normally reported in a balance-sheet statement.

138

in the balance sheets of banks and non-banks and are, accordingly, excluded from euro-currency market and other related statistics.

A bank's foreign-exchange position is "covered" if foreign-currency denominated spot and forward claims are matched with a corresponding amount of foreign-currency denominated spot and forward liabilities. Self-imposed, or legal, provisions concerning foreign-exchange cover which commercial banks may have to observe may apply to individual foreign currencies separately, or groups of foreign currencies, or all foreign currencies. The specification of foreign-currency assets and liabilities falling under any foreign-exchange cover regulations may vary from country to country or, in cases of self-imposed restrictions, may even vary from bank to bank. The "foreign-exchange" position usually includes foreign-currency claims on, and liabilities to, residents unless a special reference is made to "external" foreign-currency claims and liabilities. However, the term "external position" refers to all claims on, and liabilities to, non-residents whether denominated in foreign currencies or domestic currency. Chart G serves to illustrate these various inter-related definitions and concepts.

The term "uncovered", or "open", position refers to a situation where specified foreign-currency denominated spot and forward assets are not, or more than, fully matched with a corresponding amount of specified foreign-currency denominated spot and forward liabilities. An uncovered, or open, position is usually called a "long" position if the sum of specified foreign-currency assets exceeds that of corresponding liabilities; and a "short" position if the opposite in the case.

The term "swap transaction" refers to a combination of a spot and a forward foreign-exchange transaction in opposite directions, i. e. either a spot purchase of foreign exchange covered by a forward re-sale of the same foreign currency; or a spot sale of foreign exchange covered by a forward re-purchase of the same foreign currency. The deal may be made against another foreign currency or against domestic currency.

The term "inward swap" refers to a combination of a spot sale of foreign exchange and a forward re-purchase of the same foreign currency against domestic currency. If the other contracting party is a resident belonging to other than the banking sector - this could be a non-financial enterprise or the central bank - the operation appears in the balance-of-payments statistics as a net inflow of banking funds (increase in net external liabilities or decrease in net external assets of the banks); if however, the other contracting party is a non-resident bank or non-bank the decline in the banking sector's foreign-exchange holdings (spot) is offset by a corresponding decline in its domestic-currency liabilities to non-residents (spot) so that the overall external net position (spot) remains unchanged.

Correspondingly, the term "outward swap" refers to a combination of a spot purchase of foreign exchange and a forward re-sale of the same foreign currency against domestic currency. This leads to a net outflow of banking funds only if the other contracting party is a resident belonging to a sector other than the banking sector - again, this could be a non-financial enterprise or the central bank.

ANNEX   II

Selected data on international
banking

TABLE 1. EXTERNAL ASSETS AND LIABILITIES OF COMMERCIAL BANKS
IN REPORTING COUNTRIES
(US dollar billion)

COUNTRY	END OF PERIOD	EXTERNAL ASSETS			EXTERNAL LIABILITIES			NET EXTERNAL POSITION			USE OF DOMESTIC CURRENCY AS A "EURO-CURRENCY" (1)	
		TOTAL	OF WHICH IN:		TOTAL	OF WHICH IN:		TOTAL	OF WHICH IN:			
			DOMESTIC CURRENCY	FOREIGN CURRENCIES		DOMESTIC CURRENCY	FOREIGN CURRENCIES		DOMESTIC CURRENCY	FOREIGN CURRENCIES	ASSETS	LIABILITIES
Austria	1973	3.58	0.40	3.18	3.59	0.33	3.26	-0.01	0.07	-0.08	n.a.	n.a.
	1976	7.14	1.21	5.93	7.59	0.62	6.97	-0.45	0.59	-1.04	n.a.	n.a.
	1978	12.54	2.91	9.63	13.65	0.98	12.67	-1.11	1.93	-3.04	n.a.	n.a.
Belgium	1973(2)	25.61	1.16	24.45	25.64	1.80	23.84	-0.03	-0.64	0.61	0.88	0.50
	1976(2)	51.86	2.44	49.42	50.88	3.35	47.53	0.98	-0.91	1.89	1.82	1.06
	1978	34.58	2.80	31.78	38.27	4.73	33.54	-3.69	-1.93	-1.76	3.27	2.16
Luxembourg	1978	59.39	1.05	58.34	55.21	0.73	54.48	4.18	0.32	3.86	n.a.	n.a.
Denmark	1978	2.93	0.09	2.84	2.75	0.39	2.36	0.18	-0.20	0.38	n.a	n.a.
France	1973	29.48	1.85	27.63	31.87	4.51	27.36	-2.39	-2.66	0.27	1.76	2.13
	1976	49.44	1.45	47.99	52.47	3.81	48.66	-3.03	-2.36	-0.67	2.57	3.22
	1978	98.98	18.20	80.78	84.49	5.70	78.79	14.49	12.50	1.99	5.66	7.40
Germany	1973	14.83	8.13	6.70	15.74	9.08	6.66	-0.91	-0.95	0.04	31.41	32.02
	1976	40.23	25.90	14.33	31.11	17.38	13.73	9.12	8.52	0.60	48.68	47.23
	1978	61.12	40.35	20.77	59.10	40.23	18.88	2.01	0.12	1.89	97.43	93.08
Ireland	1978	1.51	..	1.51	1.81	..	1.81	-0.30	..	-0.30	1.8.	0.50
Italy	1973	24.60	0.79	23.81	25.69	1.82	23.87	-1.09	-1.03	-0.06	0.43	0.50
	1976	12.55	0.26	12.29	16.37	1.42	14.95	-3.82	-1.16	-2.66	0.34	0.40
	1978	22.75	0.59	22.16	29.81	2.01	27.80	-7.06	-1.42	-5.64	1.01	1.10
Netherlands	1973	10.32	0.91	9.41	10.80	1.18	9.62	-0.48	-0.27	-0.21	1.24	2.26
	1976	26.17	4.17	22.00	23.66	4.08	19.58	2.51	0.09	2.42	3.78	3.53
	1978	45.05	8.49	36.56	43.48	7.93	35.55	1.57	0.56	1.01	6.92	7.40
Sweden	1973	1.93	0.22	1.71	1.36	0.46	0.90	0.57	-0.24	0.81	n.a.	n.a.
	1976	3.73	0.81	2.92	2.96	0.67	2.29	0.77	0.14	0.63	n.a.	n.a.
	1978	4.25	0.86	3.39	5.22	0.70	4.52	-0.97	0.16	-1.13	n.a.	n.a.
Switzerland	1973	16.95	7.32	9.63	15.76	6.56	9.20	1.19	0.76	0.43	15.00	17.16
	1976	29.24	10.87	18.37	20.35	5.06	15.29	8.89	5.81	3.08	17.93	15.88
	1978	50.70	19.29	31.41	33.69	6.82	26.87	17.01	12.47	4.54	27.89	27.89
United Kingdom	1973	85.72	1.44	84.28	96.80	6.15	90.65	-11.08	-4.71	-6.37	3.08	4.56
	1976	139.80	1.80	138.00	155.75	7.13	148.62	-15.95	-5.33	-10.62	2.15	3.98
	1978	217.59	14.74	202.85	225.37	11.95	213.42	-7.78	2.79	-10.57	7.30	10.32
United States	1973	26.72	25.99	0.73	38.65	38.05	0.60	-11.93	-12.06	0.13	132.11	131.38
	1976	81.13	79.34	1.79	70.69	69.91	0.78	10.44	9.43	1.01	224.02	230.04
	1978	129.05	125.12	3.93	100.06	97.83	2.23	28.99	27.29	1.70	339.52	348.59
Canada	1973	12.34	0.40	11.94	12.62	1.09	11.53	-0.28	-0.69	0.41	0.20	0.77
	1976	17.29	0.46	16.83	16.48	1.96	14.52	0.81	-1.50	2.31	0.17	0.42
	1978	22.37	0.48	21.89	24.97	2.62	22.35	-2.60	-2.14	-0.46	0.38	0.46
Japan	1973	17.11	0.81	16.30	13.62	0.69	12.93	3.49	0.12	3.37	n.a	n.a
	1976	21.64	2.08	19.56	29.04	1.88	27.16	-7.40	0.20	-7.60	n.a	n.a
	1978	33.69	7.97	25.72	39.02	8.70	30.32	-5.33	-0.73	-4.60	n.a	n.a

(1) Assets and liabilities reported by banks located in the countries (reporting to the BIS) other than the one whose currency is used. Assets include working balances, and possibly other deposits, held with banks located in the country whose currency is used and, therefore, do not entirely consist of "euro-market" claims.

(2) Consolidated Figures for Belgium and Luxembourg.

Source: Bank for International Settlements, Annual Reports and national surces.

Table 2: RELATIVE IMPORTANCE OF SELECTED
COUNTRIES AS INTERNATIONAL
BANKING CENTRES

Country	Commercial Banks' External Assets and Liabilities as Percentage of Total (End of Period)					
	Assets			Liabilities		
	1973	1976	1979	1973	1976	1979
Austria	n.a.	n.a.	1.8	n.a.	n.a.	1.9
Belgium (1))			4.3			5.1
Luxembourg (1))	9.6	11.0	8.2	8.9	10.8	7.7
Denmark	n.a.	n.a.	0.4	n.a.	n.a.	0.4
France	11.1	10.4	12.8	11.0	11.2	10.7
Germany	5.6	8.5	7.0	5.5	6.6	7.8
Ireland	n.a.	n.a.	0.2	n.a.	n.a.	0.2
Italy	9.3	2.7	3.0	8.9	3.5	3.8
Netherlands	3.9	5.5	5.7	3.7	5.0	5.6
Sweden	0.7	0.8	0.6	0.5	0.6	0.9
Switzerland	6.4	6.2	6.0	5.5	4.4	3.9
United Kingdom	32.3	29.5	29.1	33.5	33.2	30.4
United States	10.1	17.0	13.8	13.4	15.0	13.2
Canada	4.6	3.7	2.6	4.4	3.5	3.3
Japan	6.4	4.6	4.6	4.7	6.2	5.1
Total	100.0	100.0	100.0	100.0	100.0	100.0
US $ billion	265.61	473.08	983.24	288.55	469.76	991.59

(1) 1973 and 1976: Consolidated figures for Belgium and Luxembourg.

Source: Bank for International Settlements, Annual Reports.

TABLE 3. EXTERNAL FOREIGN-CURRENCY LIABILITIES
OF COMMERCIAL BANKS
(position at end period)

	1973	1974	1975	1976	1977	1978	1979
	US dollar billion						
Austria	n.a	n.a	n.a	n.a	9.7	12.8	17.9
Belgium	11.8	15.2	15.7	19.1	23.5	33.5	43.6
Luxembourg	12.7	17.4	23.3	30.1	41.9	54.5	75.6
Denmark	n.a	n.a	n.a	n.a	1.4	2.4	3.3
France	27.4	32.5	38.1	48.7	63.0	78.8	99.6
Germany	6.7	7.7	9.3	13.7	15.2	18.9	23.4
Ireland	n.a	n.a	n.a	n.a	1.7	1.8	2.2
Italy	23.8	13.6	15.0	15.0	21.5	27.8	35.2
Netherlands	9.6	12.6	16.4	19.6	25.5	35.5	44.6
Sweden	0.9	1.0	1.8	2.3	3.4	4.5	7.8
Switzerland	9.2	10.6	12.0	15.3	18.0	26.9	30.8
United Kingdom	90.7	111.5	128.2	148.7	171.4	213.4	282.0
Sub-total	192.9	222.1	259.8	312.5	396.2	510.8	666.0
United States	0.6	0.8	0.6	0.8	0.9	2.2	2.3
Canada	11.5	11.7	12.1	14.5	16.7	22.4	29.7
Japan	12.9	24.1	25.2	27.2	24.5	30.3	46.7
Total	217.9	258.7	297.7	355.0	438.3	565.7	744.7
	Per cent of total						
Austria	n.a	n.a	n.a	n.a	2.2	2.3	2.4
Belgium	5.4	5.9	5.3	5.4	5.4	5.9	5.9
Luxembourg	5.8	6.7	7.8	8.5	9.6	9.6	10.2
Denmark	n.a	n.a	n.a	n.a	0.3	0.4	0.4
France	12.6	12.6	12.8	13.7	14.4	13.9	13.4
Germany	3.1	3.0	3.1	3.9	3.5	3.3	3.1
Ireland	n.a	n.a	n.a	n.a	0.4	0.3	0.3
Italy	11.0	5.3	5.0	4.2	4.9	4.9	4.7
Netherlands	4.4	4.9	5.5	5.5	5.8	6.3	6.0
Sweden	0.4	0.4	0.6	0.6	0.8	0.8	1.0
Switzerland	4.2	4.1	4.0	4.3	4.1	4.9	4.1
United Kingdom	41.6	43.1	43.1	41.9	39.1	37.7	37.9
Sub-total	88.5	85.9	87.3	88.0	90.4	90.3	89.4
United States	0.3	0.3	0.2	0.2	0.2	0.4	0.3
Canada	5.3	4.5	4.1	4.1	3.8	4.0	4.0
Japan	5.9	9.3	8.4	7.7	5.6	5.3	6.3
Total	100.0	100.0	100.0	100.0	100.0	100.0	100.0

Sources: Bank for International Settlements, annual reports and
national sources.

TABLE 4. RELATIVE IMPORTANCE OF MAJOR EURO-CURRENCIES

CURRENCY	EXTERNAL FOREIGN-CURRENCY LIABILITIES OF COMMERCIAL BANKS[1] (POSITION AT END-PERIOD)						
	1973	1974	1975	1976	1977	1978	1979
	per cent of total						
US dollar	68.4	70.8	73.2	74.0	70.4	68.2	65.6
Deutsche Mark	16.7	15.6	15.4	15.2	17.3	18.2	19.2
Swiss franc	8.9	8.3	5.9	5.1	5.7	5.5	6.1
Sterling	2.4	1.6	1.2	1.3	1.7	2.0	2.3
Guilder	1.1	1.3	1.4	1.1	1.3	1.4	1.3
French franc	1.1	1.0	1.3	1.0	1.1	1.4	1.7
Belgian franc	0.3	0.3	0.3	0.3	0.5	0.4)	3.8
Other	1.1	1.1	1.3	2.0	2.0	2.9)	
Total	100.0	100.0	100.0	100.0	100.0	100.0	100.0
US $ billion	192.1	220.8	258.7	310.7	396.2	510.8	666.0

(1)   Of the nine and, starting from end 1977, twelve European
        countries reporting to the Bank for International
        Settlements.

NOTE: Data for Belgium and Luxembourg are consolidated for the
        years 1973-1976 which explains the difference between sub-
        totals shown for these years in table 3 and the totals of
        table 4.

SOURCE: Bank for International Settlements, Annual Reports and
        national source.

Table 5. SELECTED MAIN CENTRES FOR MAJOR EURO-CURRENCIES

(position end-December 1978)

US $ billion

COUNTRY IN WHICH REPORTING COMMERCIAL BANKS ARE LOCATED	COMMERCIAL BANKS' EXTERNAL FOREIGN-CURRENCY LIABILITIES DENOMINATED IN:						
	US DOLLAR	DEUTSCHE MARK	SWISS FRANC	STERLING	GUILDER	FRENCH FRANC	YEN
Belgium	19.241	6.288	1.858	2.201	1.458	2066	906
Luxembourg	24.395	24.656	2.673	476	820	1021	70
France	53.165	14.453	5.848	2.269	1.147	–	351
Germany	14.507	–	2.221	712	300	259	114
Italy	21.840	3.510	1.509	170	110	467	62
Netherlands	20.710	6.494	2.162	2.620	–	830	752
Sweden	2.795	533	713	119	167	46	13
Switzerland	18.539	5.972	–	507	435	656	
United Kingdom	167.246	25.828	8.374	–	2.732	1948	3915
Canada	21.343	661	14	20	4	6	29
Total	363.781	88.395	25.372	9.094	7.173	7299	6212

Source: Bank for International Settlements and National Sources.

TABLE 6. RELATIVE IMPORTANCE OF FOREIGN BUSINESS OF COMMERCIAL BANKS

COUNTRY	END OF PERIOD	TOTAL ASSETS (=TOTAL LIABILITIES)	OF WHICH:		TOTAL	
			FOREIGN ASSETS	FOREIGN LIABILITIES	FOREIGN ASSETS	FOREIGN LIABILITIES
		billions of national currency			as per cent of TOTAL ASSETS	
AUSTRIA	1973	427.54	70.06	70.41	16.4	16.5
	1976	716.43	128.09	136.12	17.9	19.0
	1979	1135.61	242.54	257.37	21.4	22.7
BELGIUM	1973	1176.9	486.0	552.9	41.3	47.0
	1976	1776.7	773.8	860.5	43.6	48.4
	1979	2882.0	1378.9	1644.6	47.9	57.1
LUXEMBOURG	1973	715.5	656.1	588.5	91.7	82.3
	1976	1419.9	1314.5	1203.7	92.6	84.8
	1979	2737.5	2591.2	2376.6	94.7	86.8
DENMARK	1973	58.12	4.54	4.81	7.8	8.3
	1976	85.58	10.66	8.67	12.5	10.1
	1979	114.93	26.27	23.81	22.9	20.7
FRANCE	1973	659.68	148.32	154.31	22.5	23.4
	1976	1015.82	205.21	255.94	20.2	25.2
	1979	1753.81	496.08	421.64	28.3	24.0
GERMANY	1973	863.5	58.0	42.1	6.7	4.9
	1976	1155.9	116.4	71.3	10.1	6.2
	1979	1565.4	146.5	132.8	9.4	8.5
IRELAND (millions of Irish pounds)	1973	2059.1	825.7	841.2	40.1	40.9
	1976	3464.4	1380.2	1399.5	39.8	40.4
	1979	6250.9	2477.5	2611.2	39.6	41.8
ITALY	1973	92222	15377	15758	16.7	17.1
	1976	149970	13032	14712	8.7	9.8
	1979	265705	25489	29795	9.6	11.2
NETHERLANDS	1973	114.64	34.30	30.81	29.9	26.9
	1976	188.08	62.63	55.59	33.3	29.6
	1979	319.78	108.70	107.29	34.0	33.6
SPAIN	1973	3914	219	278	5.6	7.1
	1976	7229	249	540	3.4	7.5
	1979	11818	697	1269	5.9	10.7

TABLE 6. RELATIVE IMPORTANCE OF FOREIGN BUSINESS
OF COMMERCIAL BANKS

(Continued)

COUNTRY	END OF PERIOD	TOTAL ASSETS (=TOTAL LIABILITIES)	OF WHICH:		TOTAL	
			FOREIGN ASSETS	FOREIGN LIABILITIES	FOREIGN ASSETS	FOREIGN LIABILITIES
		billion of national currency			as per cent of TOTAL ASSETS	
SWEDEN	1973	105.74	10.14	6.28	9.6	5.9
	1976	142.13	17.39	13.33	12.2	9.4
	1979	232.67	25.07	35.79	10.8	15.4
SWITZERLAND	1973	276.6	95.8	81.0	34.6	29.3
	1976	347.7	122.1	96.6	35.1	27.8
	1979	438.2	159.2	117.3	36.3	26.8
UNITED KINGDOM (millions of pound sterling)	1973	75994	38134	41419	50.2	54.5
	1976	138314	85529	90767	61.8	65.6
	1979	200161	128678	135830	64.3	67.9
UNITED STATES	1973	722.9	24.5	40.0	3.4	5.5
	1976	926.2	75.7	71.1	8.2	7.7
	1979	1321.8	144.1	151.0	10.9	11.4
CANADA	1973	63.16	11.90	11.49	18.8	18.2
	1976	100.31	16.93	14.65	16.9	14.6
	1979	168.09	29.19	34.68	17.4	20.6
JAPAN	1973	116652	3080	4148	2.6	3.6
	1976	170258	4402	8743	2.6	5.1
	1979	234032	6168	10342	2.6	4.4

Source: International Monetary Fund: International Financial Statistics; these data exclude domestic interbank deposits.

Swiss Nationalbank: Annual Reports on "Swiss banking in the year ...."; data for Switzerland include domestic interbank deposits.

OECD SALES AGENTS
DÉPOSITAIRES DES PUBLICATIONS DE L'OCDE

ARGENTINA – ARGENTINE
Carlos Hirsch S.R.L., Florida 165, 4° Piso (Galería Guemes)
1333 BUENOS AIRES, Tel. 33.1787.2391 y 30.7122

AUSTRALIA – AUSTRALIE
Australia and New Zealand Book Company Pty, Ltd.,
10 Aquatic Drive, Frenchs Forest, N.S.W. 2086
P.O. Box 459, BROOKVALE, N.S.W. 2100

AUSTRIA – AUTRICHE
OECD Publications and Information Center
4 Simrockstrasse 5300 BONN. Tel. (0228) 21.60.45
Local Agent/Agent local :
Gerold and Co., Graben 31, WIEN 1. Tel. 52.22.35

BELGIUM – BELGIQUE
LCLS
35, avenue de Stalingrad, 1000 BRUXELLES. Tel. 02.512.89.74

BRAZIL – BRÉSIL
Mestre Jou S.A., Rua Guaipa 518,
Caixa Postal 24090, 05089 SAO PAULO 10. Tel. 261.1920
Rua Senador Dantas 19 s/205-6, RIO DE JANEIRO GB.
Tel. 232.07.32

CANADA
Renouf Publishing Company Limited,
2182 St. Catherine Street West,
MONTRÉAL, Quebec H3H 1M7. Tel. (514)937.3519
522 West Hasting,
VANCOUVER, B.C. V6B 1L6. Tel. (604) 687.3320

DENMARK – DANEMARK
Munksgaard Export and Subscription Service
35, Nørre Søgade
DK 1370 KØBENHAVN K. Tel. +45.1.12.85.70

FINLAND – FINLANDE
Akateeminen Kirjakauppa
Keskuskatu 1, 00100 HELSINKI 10. Tel. 65.11.22

FRANCE
Bureau des Publications de l'OCDE,
2 rue André-Pascal, 75775 PARIS CEDEX 16. Tel. (1) 524.81.67
Principal correspondant :
13602 AIX-EN-PROVENCE : Librairie de l'Université.
Tel. 26.18.08

GERMANY – ALLEMAGNE
OECD Publications and Information Center
4 Simrockstrasse 5300 BONN Tel. (0228) 21.60.45

GREECE – GRÈCE
Librairie Kauffmann, 28 rue du Stade,
ATHÈNES 132. Tel. 322.21.60

HONG-KONG
Government Information Services,
Sales and Publications Office, Baskerville House, 2nd floor,
13 Duddell Street, Central. Tel. 5.214375

ICELAND – ISLANDE
Snaebjörn Jönsson and Co., h.f.,
Hafnarstraeti 4 and 9, P.O.B. 1131, REYKJAVIK.
Tel. 13133/14281/11936

INDIA – INDE
Oxford Book and Stationery Co. :
NEW DELHI, Scindia House. Tel. 45896
CALCUTTA, 17 Park Street. Tel. 240832

INDONESIA – INDONÉSIE
PDIN-LIPI, P.O. Box 3065/JKT., JAKARTA, Tel. 583467

IRELAND – IRLANDE
TDC Publishers – Library Suppliers
12 North Frederick Street, DUBLIN 1 Tel. 744835-749677

ITALY – ITALIE
Libreria Commissionaria Sansoni :
Via Lamarmora 45, 50121 FIRENZE. Tel. 579751
Via Bartolini 29, 20155 MILANO. Tel. 365083
Sub-depositari :
Editrice e Libreria Herder,
Piazza Montecitorio 120, 00 186 ROMA. Tel. 6794628
Libreria Hoepli, Via Hoepli 5, 20121 MILANO. Tel. 865446
Libreria Lattes, Via Garibaldi 3, 10122 TORINO. Tel. 519274
La diffusione delle edizioni OCSE è inoltre assicurata dalle migliori
librerie nelle città più importanti.

JAPAN – JAPON
OECD Publications and Information Center,
Landic Akasaka Bldg., 2-3-4 Akasaka,
Minato-ku, TOKYO 107 Tel. 586.2016

KOREA – CORÉE
Pan Korea Book Corporation,
P.O. Box n° 101 Kwangwhamun, SÉOUL. Tel. 72.7369

LEBANON – LIBAN
Documenta Scientifica/Redico,
Edison Building, Bliss Street, P.O. Box 5641, BEIRUT.
Tel. 354429 – 344425

MALAYSIA – MALAISIE
and/et SINGAPORE - SINGAPOUR
University of Malaysia Co-operative Bookshop Ltd.
P.O. Box 1127, Jalan Pantai Baru
KUALA LUMPUR. Tel. 51425, 54058, 54361

THE NETHERLANDS – PAYS-BAS
Staatsuitgeverij
Verzendboekhandel Chr. Plantijnnstraat
S-GRAVENAGE. Tel. nr. 070.789911
Voor bestellingen: Tel. 070.789208

NEW ZEALAND – NOUVELLE-ZÉLANDE
Publications Section,
Government Printing Office,
WELLINGTON: Walter Street. Tel. 847.679
Mulgrave Street, Private Bag. Tel. 737.320
World Trade Building, Cubacade, Cuba Street. Tel. 849.572
AUCKLAND: Hannaford Burton Building,
Rutland Street, Private Bag. Tel. 32.919
CHRISTCHURCH: 159 Hereford Street, Private Bag. Tel. 797.142
HAMILTON: Alexandra Street, P.O. Box 857. Tel. 80.103
DUNEDIN: T & G Building, Princes Street, P.O. Box 1104.
Tel. 778.294

NORWAY – NORVÈGE
J.G. TANUM A/S Karl Johansgate 43
P.O. Box 1177 Sentrum OSLO 1. Tel. (02) 80.12.60

PAKISTAN
Mirza Book Agency, 65 Shahrah Quaid-E-Azam, LAHORE 3.
Tel. 66839

PHILIPPINES
National Book Store, Inc.
Library Services Division, P.O. Box 1934, MANILA.
Tel. Nos. 49.43.06 to 09, 40.53.45, 49.45.12

PORTUGAL
Livraria Portugal, Rua do Carmo 70-74,
1117 LISBOA CODEX. Tel. 360582/3

SPAIN – ESPAGNE
Mundi-Prensa Libros, S.A.
Castello 37, Apartado 1223, MADRID-1. Tel. 275.46.55
Libreria Bastinos, Pelayo 52, BARCELONA 1. Tel. 222.06.00

SWEDEN – SUÈDE
AB CE Fritzes Kungl Hovbokhandel,
Box 16 356, S 103 27 STH, Regeringsgatan 12,
DS STOCKHOLM. Tel. 08/23.89.00

SWITZERLAND – SUISSE
OECD Publications and Information Center
4 Simrockstrasse 5300 BONN. Tel. (0228) 21.60.45
Local Agents/Agents locaux
Librairie Payot, 6 rue Grenus, 1211 GENÈVE 11. Tel. 022.31.89.50
Freihofer A.G., Weinbergstr. 109, CH-8006 ZÜRICH.
Tel. 01.3624282

TAIWAN – FORMOSE
National Book Company,
84-5 Sing Sung South Rd, Sec. 3, TAIPEI 107. Tel. 321.0698

THAILAND – THAILANDE
Suksit Siam Co., Ltd., 1715 Rama IV Rd,
Samyan, BANGKOK 5. Tel. 2511630

UNITED KINGDOM – ROYAUME-UNI
H.M. Stationery Office, P.O.B. 569,
LONDON SE1 9NH. Tel. 01.928.6977, Ext. 410 or
49 High Holborn, LONDON WC1V 6 HB (personal callers)
Branches at: EDINBURGH, BIRMINGHAM, BRISTOL,
MANCHESTER, CARDIFF, BELFAST.

UNITED STATES OF AMERICA – ÉTATS-UNIS
OECD Publications and Information Center, Suite 1207,
1750 Pennsylvania Ave., N.W. WASHINGTON D.C.20006.
Tel. (202) 724.1857

VENEZUELA
Libreria del Este, Avda. F. Miranda 52, Edificio Galipan,
CARACAS 106. Tel. 32.23.01/33.26.04/33.24.73

YUGOSLAVIA – YOUGOSLAVIE
Jugoslovenska Knjiga, Terazije 27, P.O.B. 36, BEOGRAD.
Tel. 621.992

Les commandes provenant de pays où l'OCDE n'a pas encore désigné de dépositaire peuvent être adressées à :
OCDE, Bureau des Publications, 2, rue André-Pascal, 75775 PARIS CEDEX 16.

Orders and inquiries from countries where sales agents have not yet been appointed may be sent to:
OECD, Publications Office, 2 rue André-Pascal, 75775 PARIS CEDEX 16.

63672-2-1981

OECD PUBLICATIONS, 2, rue André-Pascal, 75775 PARIS CEDEX 16 - No. 41865 1981
PRINTED IN FRANCE
(950 TH 21 81 01 1) ISBN 92-64-12196-X